✓4/03

✓4/03

Getting Started in Science Fairs

Other books by Phyllis J. Perry, Ed.D.

A Teacher's Science Companion

Getting Started in
Science Fairs
From planning to judging

Phyllis J. Perry, Ed.D.

Illustrations by Debra Ellinger

TAB Books
Division of McGraw-Hill
New York San Francisco Washington, D.C. Auckland Bogotá Caracas Lisbon London Madrid
Mexico City Mil   Montreal New Delhi San Juan Singapore Sydney Tokyo Toronto

McGraw-Hill

*A Division of The **McGraw·Hill** Companies*

 This book is printed on recycled paper containing a minimum of 50% total recycled fiber with 15% postconsumer fiber.

pbk   2 3 4 5 6 7 8 9 10 BBC/BBC 9 9 8 7 6

Library of Congress Cataloging-in-Publication Data
Perry, Phyllis Jean.
   Getting started in science fairs : from planning to judging / by
Phyllis J. Perry.
      p.   cm.
   Includes index.
   ISBN 0-07-049526-2
   1. Science—Exhibitions—Study and teaching (Elementary)
2. Science projects—Study and teaching (Elementary) 3. Science-
-Exhibitions—Juvenile literature. 4. Science projects—Juvenile
literature. [1. Science—Exhibitions. 2. Science projects.
3. Science—Experiments. 4. Experiments.] I. Title.
Q182.3.P47 1995
507.8—dc20   94-44103
                                                                      CIP
                                                                       AC

Acquisitions editor: Kimberly Tabor
Editorial team: Robert E. Ostrander, Executive Editor
               Sally Anne Glover, Book Editor
Production team: Katherine G. Brown, Director
               Ollie Harmon, Coding
               Janice Stottlemyer, Computer Artist
               Wanda S. Ditch, Desktop Operator
               Lorie L. White, Proofreading
               Jodi L. Tyler, Indexer
Design team: Jaclyn J. Boone, Designer   SFP2
            Kathryn Stefanski, Associate Designer   0495262

For Paul and all the folks at Martin Park Elementary School in Boulder, Colorado who taught me about great science fairs! And for David, who helped every step of the way!

Contents

Introduction

There are as many reasons for holding an elementary school science fair as there are entrants! Of prime importance is the fact that a science fair is a wonderful opportunity to spark original and creative thinking in students, to promote long-term investigations involving higher-level thinking skills, and to proudly share the results with your community.

Anyone who has recently read a magazine or newspaper, watched a television program, or engaged in a conversation over the backyard fence or at the supermarket knows that locally and nationally there has been increased concern about the quality of education in the United States. It seems to be a constant topic of conversation everywhere.

The great debate is not about whether we need to improve our educational system. Almost everyone recognizes that need. Calls for reform are rampant. The debate centers around how we should go about the task. Each decade faces new challenges, offers new approaches to educating youth, and is met with new criticism.

Eight national educational goals have been proposed to be achieved by the year 2000. One of these goals flatly states that by the year 2000, U.S. students will be number one in the world in math and science achievement. In trying to meet this goal, there is a renewed focus on assessment and an increased interest in how students' math, science, and computing skills stack up against world-class standards.

This emphasis on math and science has led many schools, both elementary and secondary, public and private, to expend considerable energy and resources on science fairs as one means of stimulating interest and showcasing results to an interested public that is demanding accountability.

Many teachers find that the elementary school science fair sparks a special effort in some students to do their best. Unlike routine classroom activities such as the perennial science notebook that records experiments and observations, which is shared only with a teacher, a science fair is a special, public event.

Each project is put out for parents, other relatives, friends, teachers, and fellow students to observe. Knowing that one's work will be on display is a powerful motivator for many students.

Good public relations are important to schools. It is the public that must support the schools through taxes and bonds. Many citizens who vote on school issues have no children currently attending schools. They rely on newspaper accounts and public events for their information about what is happening in today's schools. A science fair is an opportunity to invite all interested people in the community to come into schools and see for themselves just what is going on.

The elementary school science fair is also a means of giving public recognition to dedicated science students who have tackled and carried out challenging tasks. This recognition is on a scale with the praise that some students receive at concerts, play performances, art shows, and sporting events. It is yet another means of applauding the gifts and talents of youth.

Science fairs are usually judged by science experts in the community. This is another motivator for students, who know that they will have time to discuss their projects with judges who are interested and knowledgeable in subjects dear to students' hearts. In some cases, this meeting between an experienced and a junior scientist is the beginning of a long friendship and mentorship.

As science fair participants attend the exhibits, they have the opportunity to share their ideas with other interested students and community members. And they also learn a good deal from viewing the other projects on display. Students broaden their own knowledge and understanding by studying other entries and talking with other entrants at the science fair.

Necessary considerations

Having indicated the importance of elementary school science fairs and the many benefits they offer, it's also appropriate to mention at this point that such fairs must be kept in perspective. Not all experiences associated with science fairs have been positive.

There are parents and students who can relate sad stories about their frustrations over confusion with the rules and regulations of the fair, which led to an exhibit being disqualified. There are judges who will say that a prize-winning exhibit was clearly not the work of a student but rather of one of the student's parents. There are teachers who complain that the fair was overemphasized or underemphasized.

A good elementary school science fair does not "just happen." It takes pre-planning, excellent communication, and the cooperation of many people who are involved. Some schools have a long-standing tradition of holding science fairs. These successful fairs take place each year and are an exciting and significant event in the life of the school. It looks easy. Fine-tuning might take place from year to year, but the fair is well established. In these cases, you can be sure that the major considerations relating to purposes and procedures surrounding the fair have already been thought through and decisions carefully made.

In other elementary schools, holding a science fair might be something new. And in those cases, an introduction to the whole idea of a science fair can be especially helpful. In these situations, considerable thought must be given to setting up the basic guidelines that will need to be followed during the first year.

This first year's effort should be thought of as a learning experience for all. There are sure to be mistakes. A planned evaluation process needs to be built in so that the needed modifications can be made for subsequent years.

Picking a date that fits with the school calendar and coincides with districtwide fairs will be relatively easy. So will finding a spot well in advance that can be reserved to house the many exhibits. Locating sufficient judges is a challenge, but it can be accomplished if the planning committee starts early enough.

There are other decisions that will be more difficult because they involve value judgments and require consensus among many people. Typical of these latter types of issues is whether entry in the fair should be voluntary or required.

Some schools require each student to enter a project in the science fair. Each science fair project is assessed, and that assessment is included as part of the student's science grade. In other schools, entry into the fair is entirely voluntary. And in some schools, there might be a blend. For example, intermediate students might be required to enter the fair, while primary grade students are invited to participate as individuals or groups.

Decisions of this sort should be made after careful and thoughtful discussion among all those involved. It might be that teachers in the intermediate grades, with support of school administrators and with buy-in from parents and students, will decide to require entry into the fair. Or they might decide that entry in the fair is voluntary. In either case, they might want to implement whichever decision they make for a couple of years and then revisit the issue.

A decision to require intermediate students to participate is often based on the belief that students in grades four through six have sufficient maturity to carry out a long-term, independent-study project and will benefit from doing so. Teachers are willing to commit valuable class time to providing the kinds of support discussed in detail in chapter 2, "The teacher's role in the elementary school science fair." Parents might indicate a willingness to be supportive in the ways outlined in chapter 3, "The parent's role in the elementary school science fair."

It is common for parents of young students and for primary-grade teachers to decide that entry into the elementary school science fair will be by student interest only and will not be required. Participation of younger students might be enhanced by providing opportunity for students to team with others from different grades to enter a joint project in the fair.

Sometimes primary-grade teachers model the way a science fair project should be done and stimulate student interest in the current and future fairs by having the entire class work on a group project, which is then entered as a special exhibit in the fair.

Another area of consideration that needs attention is the judging of entries of projects in the fair and the prizes, if any, to be awarded. It is common in elementary schools to provide a participant's ribbon and certificate to each student who enters the fair. This serves as a recognition of effort and signifies that all students are "winners."

In some cases, a few elementary school science projects are singled out to receive "special awards of merit" or to go on to district competition. The thinking here parallels student recognition in other fields. At a vocal concert, for example, some exceptional students are showcased as "solo" numbers. In athletics, some outstanding students are selected as "all-stars." Some people believe that in science fairs, the work of some students should be designated for special distinction.

School district policies might dictate whether or not elementary school science fair projects are eligible to go on for further judging. Whatever the policies and procedures to be followed, they should be announced well ahead of the fair.

If "winning projects" are designated to go on to district, state, or even national competition, it can certainly be an exciting and satisfying experience for the young scientists involved. But "winning" is not the most important aspect of the fair. Recognizing this fact, many elementary schools choose not to send projects on for further competition.

Far more important than "winning" is the fact that elementary school science fairs provide an opportunity for gaining experience in the practical application of carrying out scientific research. The student's chosen project might be a rather simple experiment. But by going through the steps of planning, hypothesizing, developing appropriate procedures, gathering data, and finally drawing conclusions, the student has been involved in a very valuable learning experience. Rather than mere rote learning, higher-level thinking skills have been brought into play.

Once a decision is made to hold an elementary school science fair, and the general decisions regarding procedures to be followed have been decided through discussion and consensus, a science fair committee needs to be set up in the building to do the detailed planning and work that is necessary for success. If at all possible, parents, as well as teachers, should serve on this science fair committee. Student representation on the committee is also an excellent idea.

Objectives of an elementary school science fair

If a decision has been made to hold an elementary school science fair, chances are good that those involved in making that decision have a number of objectives in mind. Although they might be worded in different ways, common objectives include:

➤ To stimulate student interest in science and mathematics.

➤ To provide students with educational opportunities experienced through direct participation in scientific research.

➤ To publicly recognize the work that students have done by carrying out their projects to completion.

➤ To provide students with the opportunity to share what they have learned with other students and community members.

Purpose of this guidebook

This book helps to clarify the roles of teachers, parents, and students. It also provides information about types of projects, the scientific method, and practical tips, including possible topics for research. Included are short bibliographies, sample forms (which can be photocopied), and a chapter devoted to exhibiting and judging at the fair.

Whether your interest in this book stems from being a student, parent, teacher, or judge, and whether you are approaching your first science fair or your fifteenth, it is hoped that this book will be a helpful tool in ensuring a successful and satisfying elementary school science fair.

Symbols used in this book

adult supervision

electricity

sharp object

animal safety/proper handling of animals and insects

fire

scissors

stove

dangerous chemical

1
Tips to students

So you've decided to do a project and enter the school science fair. Good for you! With preplanning and some hard work on your part, the days ahead will be fun and exciting. Your teacher and your parents will probably be of help and support to you, but the bulk of the responsibility for the project rests on your shoulders. Realizing this, you need to carefully organize and budget your time and resources.

Many of your friends might already know exactly what projects they want to do. As soon as the fair is announced, they might start immediately. This might work out well for them. But don't feel that you have to plunge in until you are ready.

It's all too easy to leap right into a project with enthusiasm only to find out in a few days (or weeks or months) that you made a crucial error at the outset. This can be costly in both time and resources. Unless, due to a long-term interest, you already know exactly what sort of project you want to undertake, you should take your time to carefully consider your possibilities.

This might be the first major independent-study project that you've done. Perhaps you're entering the science fair because it's required at school, and your project will represent a large part of your science grade. You might be entering because you're really interested in some branch of science and see this as an opportunity to further your investigations and share what you learn. Or perhaps you have no special idea for a project, but a science fair sounds like fun, and you want to be a part of it.

Whatever your reasons for entering the fair, it's wise to realize at the outset that it's going to take time and hard work. You can't wait until the weekend before the fair and then turn your attention to it and expect to have a worthwhile completed project. So as soon as you decide to enter, begin to plan.

First you're going to have to decide on a topic and the type of project you want to do. Chapter 5 of this book will help you to investigate the various possibilities: comparative surveys, controlled experiments, simple experiments, demonstrations of a scientific principle or a complex natural phenomenon, preparing a collection, or making a model.

While you are exploring topics, you might come up with an idea that you've never thought of before. It intrigues you, and you want to learn more about it. Or perhaps an interest you once had but dropped some time ago will attract you again. In this early stage, you can be open to many possibilities. It's like being hungry and looking over a huge buffet. Exactly what do you want to put on your plate?

Even though you haven't committed yourself and are still only exploring possible topics, you're going to have to do some initial research. Perhaps you'll do some reading in the library. Maybe you'll have to interview some experts in the field. You might need to go on a field trip to see how a fish hatchery works, or what happens at a water treatment plant, etc. This initial research might help you to focus your project on a specific topic in a broad area in which you are interested.

Your teacher might require you to do a background research paper as part of your science fair project. Or you might simply have to write up and present a few pages attached to your display board that tell the purpose of your project, your hypothesis, your gathered data, and your conclusions. Either way, you'll want to be sure that your work is scientifically accurate and that the spelling, grammar, and sentence structure in your paper are correct.

If you are carrying out an investigation for your project study, you'll want to follow the scientific method discussed in detail in chapter 4. You'll want to be sure that you follow your procedures carefully and safely and that you make accurate measurements and observations. Then you'll need to tabulate and write up your conclusions. Having a time line to guide you throughout your investigation will also be important. Without these, you might find that you do not have enough data or enough time to consider and write your conclusions.

If you are demonstrating a scientific law or a complex natural phenomenon, you can still pattern your project using the steps involved in the scientific method. Using some specific application of the law or an example of the phenomenon, you can write an hypothesis. For example, if you want to demonstrate that the weight of a falling object does not determine the speed at which it falls, you can gather a number of objects and demonstrate this law in your science fair project setting. Under these circumstances, though, you will know ahead of time what the conclusion will be if you follow your procedures carefully.

Some students use a computer to program a robot. Other students build a model or enter a collection in the science fair. If you are going to do this, you can make your project a better entry by considering the questions you might ask and what underlying general principle you might demonstrate through your model or your collection.

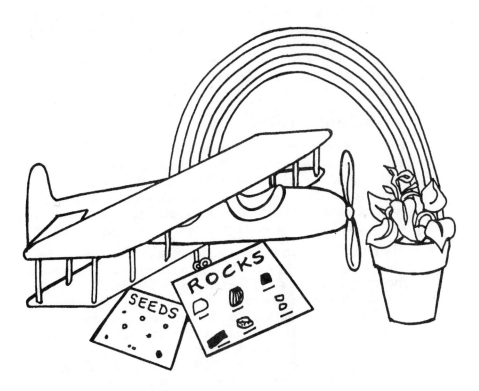

For example, if you want to enter a rock collection, you might ask questions such as these: Are all rocks equally hard? Is the hardness of a rock correlated to the density of a rock? Then you can pose an hypothesis and test it, as well as display your interesting collection.

As another example, you might already know what causes a rainbow. But can you pose some questions and think of some ways that you could demonstrate to the visitors at the science fair how one is formed? If you want to build a model airplane, can you pose some questions about the shape of airplane wings or the kinds of energy used to fly a plane, and can you demonstrate or explain the an-

swers to your questions in some way? If so, you might have the makings of a good science fair project.

If you simply bring in a collection of seeds, rocks, plants, etc., you really do not have a science fair project. You only have a collection. Going a few extra steps will help you include your collection as part of a science project. It is essential for a science fair project that you formulate an hypothesis and try to prove or illustrate it.

Sharing your data at the science fair from whichever type of project you've selected also allows you to use your artistic abilities. What color will your background display board be? Will you hand letter or type results? Will pictures, drawings, graphs, or charts help make your display more informational and more appealing? You might also be showing off your language arts and math abilities through the background research paper that you write and through the observations and measurements you record while carrying out your investigation.

And finally, when your entry is finished and on display at the fair, you'll have the satisfaction of knowing that you planned and carried out a lengthy project, brought it to completion, and learned and used a lot of skills in the process. Now that you've had an overview of the whole process of the elementary school science fair, you'll want to look into the details and get going!

Selecting a topic

Choose something that you enjoy and that is of real interest to you for your science fair project. This might be the most valuable piece of advice that you read in this book. Your science fair project will probably take you many weeks to complete. You'll have to read, question, collect data, formulate hypotheses, test your hypotheses, and come up with conclusions. You'll be devoting a lot of time and energy to this, so choose a topic that has "staying power" for you!

The general categories will be outlined by your school science fair committee. These categories might vary a little from school to school or state to state, but they are generally the same. The categories will include: botany (plants, agriculture, forestry); earth science (geology, geography, meteorology, conservation, global changes, extinctions); engineering (electrical, mechanical, chemical, aeronautical studies); health and behavioral science (human health, psychology, health hazards, and behaviors); mathematics and computer science; microbiology (molds, bacteria, protozoa); physical science (physics, chemistry, astronomy); and zoology (animal growth, animal behavior, paleontology).

Perhaps you already have an idea for your project in mind. If so, ask yourself into which of the categories does your idea fit. Look up that category in one of the following chapters of this book. If you don't have an idea yet, browsing through the various sections in chapters 6 through 13 might spark some possibilities of real interest to you.

You might get an idea for your science fair project from questions that come up in a class discussion. Perhaps there will be an issue included in your local paper or a magazine that you read that seems interesting to you and worth exploring. A topic might appear as a subject of a television program or a movie.

Perhaps you are experiencing some wild weather, or there has been a fire or other natural disaster in your area. Maybe your community is facing some real problem such as smog or a water shortage. Any of these things might provide you with a reason to do some study.

Talk over your ideas with friends and relatives and local experts. They might shed additional insights and raise issues you hadn't thought of. But before making a final choice of a project, be sure that it is one you care about. Also try to give your project a "catchy" title that will help create interest when that happy day arrives for you to display it at the fair.

You want to also be sure that you will have sufficient time, resources, and support to carry out the research you have in mind. Ask yourself the following questions: In the time that I have, can I get the information I need? Is the project narrow enough in scope so that I can successfully complete it in the time allowed? Will I need help from others? If so, are those people available to help me? Have I asked these resource people if they have the time and are willing to help?

If I need equipment or supplies, do I have them at home or at school, or can I borrow or buy what I need? Have I checked this out with my parents or others who own these tools or supplies? Have I realistically estimated all the costs involved (including art supplies for the display), and can I afford to successfully carry out this project?

You also want to consider space and safety factors. Where will you work? Where will you store things? Have you cleared this with your parents or others who are involved? Are you using any dangerous substances or unstable compounds? Do you have needed safety gear such as goggles? Is the electrical circuit you'll be using appropriate for your experiments? Do you need permits of any kind?

Many elementary school science fairs do not permit the use of live animals in projects or the display of animals at the fair. Even if animals are permitted, their use might cause additional concerns. You should be aware that animal rights lobbies might get involved if you use live vertebrates.

You also need to know that some types of laboratory animals are cannibalistic. You must take special care of any animals you are observing. You might be asked to explain any deaths that occur during your experiments. For all these reasons, it is suggested that you not use live animals in your elementary school science fair project.

However, if you do decide to involve animals in your project, be sure before you begin that such an experiment would be accepted by your school science fair committee and that you have parental approval. You also need to be certain that you have enough available specimens, room to keep them, and homes for them after the fair unless you plan to keep them yourself over a long term.

If there is a chance of exhibits going from your local school to a district, state, or national fair, and if you are using live animals, you'll want to check with the Science Service in Washington, D.C. to be sure you meet all of its standards. It would be disappointing after all your efforts to find out that your entry is being disqualified.

After you've spent some time browsing in the library and talking about science fair ideas with your teachers, friends, and relatives, and after you've considered all the aspects involved, you should finally come up with a general topic and a purpose for your science fair project.

Discuss your tentative decision with your parents and listen to their suggestions. Then discuss it with your teacher, who will probably need to sign off on your project registration form. Again, be open to suggestions. Ask yourself: Does this project idea still sound exciting to me? Will it be useful to know? Can I make it understandable to others? Can I afford it? Have I thought of a "catchy title?" Once you answer these questions, if the project still sounds good to you, you're ready to begin.

Developing and following a project schedule

The old saying goes that, "Time flies when you're having fun." It also flies when you're working on a science fair project. To avoid last-minute panic, make a schedule of due dates and intermediate steps that must be taken. You can record this on a sheet of paper or even on a desk calendar that allows you enough room to write in information.

Although each science investigation has unique needs, in general your project schedule should include the following: when you are going to the library to do research; when you will phone to make appointments with people you need to meet or sites you need to visit; when you will keep those appointments or make those visits; when you will obtain necessary signatures to enter the project in the fair; when you will purchase supplies and set them up; when you will record, graph, and chart data; when you will have a completed bibliography; when you will have finished writing up your project; the date when the final project is due; how and when it will be transported to school; whom you will invite to attend the fair and celebrate with you!

Science fair time schedule

Your science fair time schedule might look something like Table 1-1.

Table 1-1 Science Fair Time Schedule

Date:	Activity
9/15	Receive announcement of the school science fair. Browse through chapters 7 through 14 of this book. Discuss possible topics with my friends and teachers. Discuss possibilities with other interested adults. Begin my log/notebook and make regular entries.
10/1	Prepare on a card the question that I wish to answer by completing my science project and submitting this question to my teacher for approval. Begin reading and research. Keep bibliography on index cards of books and magazines that I consult. Take notes from my reading and interviews. Make entries in log/notebook.
11/1	Write a draft of my project paper OR Write a draft of my purpose, hypothesis, procedures, and how I plan to handle data. Make entries in log/notebook.
12/1	Make final decisions and revise my project paper OR Revise into final form my purpose, hypothesis, procedures, and how I will handle data. Purchase needed supplies and materials and set up my investigation. Make entries in log/notebook.
1/1	Carry out my investigation. Make entries in log/notebook.
2/1	Continue with investigation. Make entries in log/notebook.
3/1	Complete registration for science fair with signatures of my teacher and my parents, and turn it in to science fair committee.
3/5	Prepare results and conclusions from my project. Prepare any graphs, charts, tables.
3/10	Have project paper complete in final form. Have display board complete in final form.
3/15	Attend the elementary school science fair.
3/25	Attend the district science fair.

Keeping a log and project notebook

You will probably need to keep a project log or notebook. The project log could be kept in a spiral notebook, or you could use lined sheets of paper added to a three-ring binder, divided into sections, something like Table 1-2.

Table 1-2 Project Log

Date:	Time:	Activity
9/16	7–9 P.M.	At local library reading about carnivorous plants.
9/17	10–11 A.M.	Visit to Green Nursery to discuss carnivorous plants with Jim Brown.
9/17	3–4 P.M.	Reading, taking notes, and writing bibliography cards.
9/20	4–5 P.M.	Reading catalogues on where to buy plant specimens.

Although each entry in a project log/notebook is short, it is important. This log will provide you with accurate information on how you invested your time in your project. Often the log is turned in with the final project. Your teacher might provide you will a special form to follow, or you might be asked to develop your own format something like the one shown in Table 1-2.

Carrying out an investigation and/or constructing an exhibit

The details of carrying out your science fair investigation will be discussed in chapters 4 and 5. Even though you have your topic and some interesting questions, you still need to decide whether you will choose an investigation with simple experiments, controlled experiments, or surveys, or whether you will do a demonstration or present a collection or a model. Reading these two chapters carefully will help you on your way.

Once you've made your decisions about the details of your investigation, you need to set to work. Purchase or gather the supplies you need. Set them up in a safe place. Continue with your reading and research. Make accurate entries in your project log. Follow your time schedule so that there is time for growth of seeds, the erosion of soil, the fading of fabrics, or whatever is called for in your particular investigation.

Taking notes and making a bibliography

During the time that you are actually carrying out your research, you will continue to read and learn more about your subject. Each time that you read an article in a magazine or a chapter in a book, be sure to add it to your bibliography. There are many possibilities for doing this, but an easy way is to use index cards.

On each index card, list the following information: the title of the book or title of the article and title of the magazine; the author(s), the page numbers of the magazine article or section of the book; the copyright date of the book or the month and year of the magazine; and the publisher. You might want to look at the bibliographies included in this book to see examples of acceptable forms.

If you are using a short quote from the book or magazine in your science project paper, you can write the quote on the back of the same index card, listing the page number and checking to see that you have quoted exactly. If you are go-

ing to use a long quote or paraphrase some of the ideas and research, you'll want to use note paper and list the author and title in your notes.

While this might seem like a lot of work at the time, the effort you invest pays off when it comes time to write your background research paper. If a separate bibliography is required by your teacher, you can shuffle your cards into alphabetical order by author's name and easily make your list.

It's surprising that even though you are sure you will remember in what chapter and what book or magazine you came across an interesting fact, in time you might forget. Since your first reading, you might have read additional information in a number of different books and magazines. It's very annoying and time-consuming to spend a lot of time to search again for something of interest that you've recently read. If you have jotted down information in your notes or on an index card, it's very easy to relocate it.

Your classroom teacher will probably provide a lot of help about how to write your science project paper. Follow these guidelines carefully. For general information on how to go about a paper, you might want to consult chapter 2 of this book, where the process is discussed in detail.

Being ready to share and explain your project

Think about how to display the results of your investigation. Will you simply write up a conclusion, or can you show the data in a pie chart, a graph, table, or some other means? Remember that it often clarifies information to have conclusions shown in more than one format. If you are including a computer program as part of your project, you will need to prepare clear, simple directions that are "user friendly."

You will also need to follow exactly your school instructions about how to display your science fair exhibit. Usually your project will be shown on a free-standing, three-part display board. The size might vary from one school to another, so be sure you have these dimensions before you begin. You do not want to arrive at the fair and have your hard work rejected because your display board is an inch too tall or wide.

The figure below shows a diagram of a typical completed display board. Be sure to consider this a guideline only. Your teacher or school science fair committee will specify the exact dimensions that you must work within. These can vary from one elementary school building to another. Use the measurements provided by your school.

The display should be free-standing. Although oak tag board will work, it tends to be too flimsy and to fall down at an awkward moment. A heavy cardboard or other art board will be much more likely to stand up throughout the fair.

You will need to do some lettering, such as the title of your project and titles for graphs and other displays. Be sure to letter neatly and to spell correctly. While this is not just a language-arts project, your best writing skills still need to be used.

There also might be specific directions about the lettering and arrangement of print materials on your science project display board. Follow these directions. This is not the time to get in a rush or to be careless. While lettering, measure and draw a baseline (that you can erase later if you wish) to assure that your letters do not slope up or down.

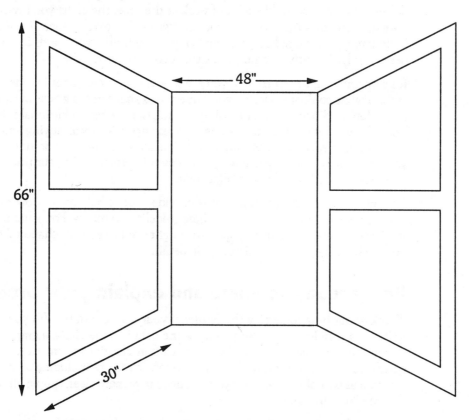

A typical science fair display board

Plan ahead with your lettering, lightly sketching each letter in place, so that you don't have good spacing in the beginning and then a crowded jumble toward the end of the line. The overall appearance of your final product should be something of which you can be proud.

Allow some time to make your display colorful and interesting. Good artwork won't make up for bad science, but it can certainly add to a good project. A colorful and artistically arranged display will catch the eye of the judges and those who come to visit the fair. These final "finishing touches" really do make a difference.

Remember that you might have to carry this project to school, so the display board should be both sturdy and lightweight. If someone from your family is going to drive you, find out ahead of time whether or not your display board will easily fit in the car. Fasten things securely. Using a brad or piece of hardware might be much better than depending on a piece of tape to hold something in place. It is discouraging to set up your display and then come back a short time later only to discover that parts have fallen off.

After completing your investigation, drawing conclusions, completing your background paper and charts, and displaying them attractively, you might think that you are finished. Not quite!

Although each elementary school science fair is handled differently, you should be prepared to do some explaining to someone about your project. In many fairs, a team of local scientists come to the school on the day of the fair and judge the exhibits. Usually, a science fair judge will take the time to speak with you individually.

Try to regard this interview about your project as an opportunity rather than a hurdle. It is not often that you get the undivided attention of a scientist who is interested in the same topics that you are. The judge will want to know why you chose this topic, how you carried out the project, what challenges you encountered, and what you learned from it all.

Some students find this interview difficult. They are nervous and either clam up and say almost nothing or develop an offhand attitude and say things they

A typical science fair display board

really don't mean. For instance, when a judge asks why you chose this topic, you could say "I don't know." Or you could answer, "I've always been interested in plants, and I grow a lot of plants at home in my room. I spent two weeks browsing through library books and magazines trying to decide what particular plant experiment I'd like to do for the school science fair."

If a judge says, "I'm not sure I understand this graph. Would you explain it to me?" You could say, "Do you need glasses or something?" Or you might answer, "Along the bottom line, I'm showing the number of days that I observed the plants, and on the vertical axis, I'm showing the height of each plant in centimeters."

You know which of the responses above is appropriate, and you can guess how a judge might react to each. Don't worry about being scared during this interview. Just remember that you've spent more time and energy on this project than anyone. You're an expert! Even the learned judge wasn't around while you were conducting your experiments. You should feel confident and should be able to explain clearly what you were trying to do, how you went about it, and what you learned.

Speak simply and to the point. Use specialized terminology only if you really understand it. The judge won't care whether you use great big words or small ones. Do you answer the question? Can you explain to others what you've studied?

Also listen for suggestions. The judge might offer some comments about what you might have done that would have given more results, or a procedure you followed that cast your results in doubt. This is not a time to argue. It is a time to learn. It might be that your next science fair project will benefit from what you are finding out right now. It might also be the case that between the school and district or regional fair, you will be allowed to make some changes and add information to your project to make it a stronger and sounder one. Properly approached, your elementary school science fair project can be a real highlight of your school year! Good luck!

2

The teacher's role in the elementary school science fair

As a teacher, perhaps you're an old hand at elementary school science fairs. If so, you might find some helpful hints and some useful forms in this book that will make the fair easier for you this year. If this is your first experience with a science fair, you might consider this to be your first science fair survival guide. It is written to help you get started in planning, doing, and judging projects at a fair.

Motivating and communicating with students and parents

One of your most important functions in connection with the fair is motivating students. While students might be motivated by the fact that in some schools science fair participation is required, and a grade given, this is not sufficient. Such requirements might generate an entry, but perhaps not much energy or enthusiasm.

Indeed, if a major portion of a grade hangs in the balance over a science project where little help and guidance is offered to the student, the fair can seem threatening and coercive. Your job as a teacher is to help turn such a "requirement" into an exciting "opportunity."

To be successful in motivating students, you need to allow ample time for a successful project to be carried out, provide for communication and buy-in with parents as well as with students, provide class time to give instructions and assistance, and demonstrate your own enthusiasm for the fair and signal its importance. With this caliber of motivation and support, every student can succeed.

Some teachers complain that many student projects at the fair "look as if they were carelessly done the night before the science fair took place." And this might be the truth. But if this is the case, teachers share some of the responsibility for these hastily done projects. Such slipshod work can be avoided by maintaining good communication and setting up some regular checkpoints.

If there is a school calendar that goes home in the beginning of the year that lists vacations, school year quarters, parent conference dates, dates for school musicals and art fairs, etc., be sure that the school science fair date is included. If you send home a letter to parents at the beginning of the school year with information about your classroom, be sure that the science fair date is listed there.

Once school is under way, sometime in the middle of September, spend some time talking about the science fair with your students, even though the fair won't be taking place until March. If you and your fellow teachers take some slides of science fair projects and activities from previous years, over time, you can put together an interesting slide show that serves as a good motivator to show to this year's crop of students.

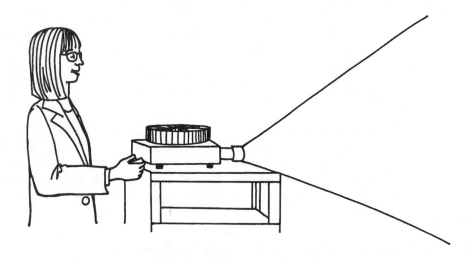

Students who watch a slide show of fairs that took place in their school in recent years will recognize some of the students, will see judges talking with young scientists, will notice crowds visiting the fair, will observe successful display boards, and might also get ideas for topics they might want to investigate. Such a show serves as an introduction and is a good motivator.

But face it, even though you project enthusiasm and great slides of previous fairs, a lot of students will hear the words "planning for the science fair that will be held next March," and tune you out. To some students, March is an eternity away. But a few in the class, often your most eager and dedicated science students, will begin to think about the fair and what sorts of long-term projects they want to investigate.

To be sure that you get every student's attention, it is wise to send home a separate sheet of information about the science fair, even though you might have mentioned it in a general classroom newsletter. This adds to the fair's importance and makes sure that information about the science fair is not lost in the crowd of other information.

Include some dates or checkpoints when the student must report to you. These might include:

➤ A definite date when the tentative purpose of each student's science fair investigation must be turned in to you on an index card (along with the question to be answered through the student investigation or a listing of the type of collection or model to be put together and displayed).

➤ A due date for a bibliography of books, magazines, and pamphlets consulted in choosing or pursuing a topic and to be used in writing the background research paper.

➤ A due date when the final title of the project and written purpose of the project is to be handed in on an index card.

➤ A date when the research paper (if required) is due.

➤ Dates when class periods will be devoted to discussion and consultation on science fair projects.

➤ The date when the student projects must be registered for the fair, complete with parent and teacher signatures.

➤ The dates when projects must be delivered to school and when the school science fair will be held.

➤ The date of the regional or district science fair. (You might want to refer to chapter 1 under "Science fair time schedule" to see what such a checklist for students might look like.)

Providing these checkpoints ensures that all students get an early start in thinking about their projects and getting engaged in the process. It also helps parents who want to be supportive to budget time to be helpful. And it guarantees that even though projects will vary widely in their quality, no project is completely and hastily done "the night before the fair!"

During the time when students are selecting their project topics, the teacher also needs to communicate in detail specific science fair regulations. If the display board needs to be a specific size, this information should go home early so that effort is not wasted in presenting findings in the wrong format. If certain material such as the bibliography or background paper must be typed or word processed on computers, or cannot be done on computer, this needs to be communicated early on. Safety information, special information about projects involving live animals, or projects involving writing computer programs, etc., all need to be included in written information for students and also sent to parents.

Advising

While some students will listen to the information and suggestions you provide, watch a slide show, take home an information/checkpoint sheet to parents, and be off and running on their science projects, others will not. Some who seemed reluctant to begin might catch fire later on.

Both the eager and reluctant students might need some advising from you, which can be carried out on those days that you have already designated as dates for discussion and consultation on the science fair projects. Some students will have trouble choosing a topic. Others might have chosen a topic that is too broad. Some will need help with how to develop procedures for carrying out an investigation. Others might not know how to keep a log or notebook.

Supporting ideas and nourishing creativity

Student advising in connection with the school science fair is not a one-shot effort. You might successfully help a student choose a topic and begin an investigation, only to have the student bog down later, get frustrated with the lack of results, or run into some other unanticipated road block. Ongoing support for ideas and steady encouragement for creative approaches to all aspects of the project need to be supplied on a regular basis.

You also must recognize when a radical about-face is in order. By specifying a time for a "tentative project topic" and another time for a "final project topic," you have already allowed opportunity for a student to change his or her mind. Knowing when a student is discouraged and simply needs support to get past a hurdle and succeed, and recognizing those other times when a student has started down the wrong path and needs to begin anew, are part of the art of teaching.

Finding resources

A common reason for students to become discouraged with a science fair project is their inability to find resources. This might be a problem in locating equipment, print references, or human resources. The classroom teacher is the key to offering support in this area.

One of the greatest assets that you, as a classroom teacher, have in finding appropriate resources for students is the school's librarian or media specialist. When handing out a calendar of events or a letter to parents specifying checkpoints with respect to the science fair, be sure to give a copy to your media specialist. This allows him or her to do advance planning and to have materials on hand that might be helpful to students. Also find the time to discuss the fair with the media specialist. The media specialist's knowledge and enthusiasm are big positives in support of a school fair.

If you are going to schedule some classroom teaching time to give help on how to write a background research paper, you might want to select a time when the school media specialist can team teach with you. The media specialist is an expert in doing computer research, in using card catalogues, in finding materials in vertical files, magazines, specialized encyclopedias, newspapers, etc.

Media specialists also sometimes have specialized listings of local community resources. They might know what scientific agencies in your community have libraries that would be open to students or have a list of employees, service club members, or other volunteers who would be willing to talk with a student on a specific project. Make use of this valuable expertise. If there are other specialists in your school district such as talented and gifted education specialists, community resources liaisons, etc., be sure to tap into these resources.

Parents in your school are another valuable resource. There might be an electrical engineer, the owner of a flower shop, a computer programmer, etc. among your parent population. If your school has a Volunteer Coordinator, this person might already have a file of parents who have indicated their willingness to work on short term projects and to volunteer time with students.

If your school does not have a Volunteer Coordinator, you might want to write a plea for volunteer time and assistance which could be included in the school newsletter to parents. Make it easy for volunteers to help. Provide a school phone number where they can call and leave their name. Include a tear-off slip in the newsletter where the parent can fill in name, phone number, and area of expertise.

Some teachers say they never get help from parents because the parents are "too busy." Often the reason more parents don't volunteer for an activity is that they haven't been given enough lead time or enough information.

Employees who aren't free to come to the school during their work hours to help with the science fair might still be willing to aid one student with a project through phone consultations or even a Saturday meeting. If there is publicity, and time for advance planning, an employee might be able to get a paid afternoon off from work as a community service gesture on the part of a company that wants to show support for schools.

And don't forget retirees and senior citizens. There might be an ideal match out there for one of your students. A senior center, a retired teachers organization, or other group might be called upon for assistance. Remember that transportation poses a problem for some older people. Offering to transport the volunteer to and from school might make the difference between having and not having someone who is able to help.

Arranging for supplies and equipment

Specific individual needs might be handled one-on-one during advising time between teacher and student. One student might need to arrange some extra computer time in the school lab to prepare part of the research paper or to write a program that will be entered into the fair. Another student might need to check out some materials from the school science lab. Yet another might need to know what hobby shop or hardware store might have supplies that are needed. Some students might need to borrow catalogues from science companies to order needed supplies.

Being available to discuss details, advise, and help locate resources is very important. So is safety. As you learn more specifics about each student's project, you can discuss and help to address safety factors. This can be crucially important. But the teacher can't and shouldn't do it all.

Helping with equipment and resource needs should be coordinated between teacher and parents. It is important to maintain a balance between what the student should undertake alone, what could be accomplished by a student working with parents, and what might be done by the teacher working with the student.

Some information and resource needs might be general enough so that you might devote a class period to working with all students. If writing of any sort is to be included as part of the science fair project, this is a natural area for some related language arts instruction.

Keeping logs, notebooks, and writing a background research paper

Part of one class period could profitably be devoted to explaining the project log and/or notebook. This explanation can be enhanced by using an overhead projector or by writing on a chart what entries in a project log/notebook should look like. (See chapter 1 for an example.) Placing such information on an overhead transparency or a chart once, and storing it for future use, will save teacher time and energy in the years ahead.

Class time will also be needed to teach students how to write a background research paper, if one is required. If teachers team teach or departmentalize, with one team or teacher largely responsible for science and another largely responsible for language arts, these background research paper lessons require team planning.

Not all elementary schools require a background research paper as part of the science project. But there are some good reasons for requiring such a paper. The present-day multidisciplinary approach to education supports having significant language arts skills and important science skills combined in a single student assignment.

Writing a research paper provides practice in one type of prose organization. Being able to gather information and to present ideas clearly in a well-organized format are valuable writing skills. In order to write a good background research paper, the student will need to find and consult many resources. Being able to find information on a topic of interest is a valuable skill for the student. And it is a skill that will continue to be of importance when the student is an adult.

The research and reading needed to write the paper doesn't just address language arts skills. It also helps students to gain insights, to understand some of the theories and related research that might have already taken place, and to narrow down a topic. It also brings into play the application of higher-level thinking skills.

Selecting a manageable topic

Helping students select a manageable topic is very important. The subject has to be one in which the student is really interested, one the student can handle, and one that is not so new that background materials will be impossible to find. The subject has to be one that can be addressed within the given time limits, one that it not too technical for the elementary student, and one that would be appropriate for a school science fair.

Keeping logs, notebooks, and writing a background research paper

Spend some time brainstorming with your class and encourage students to continue this with fellow students, parents, and other interested adults. Encourage students to be alert to ideas as they watch movies and TV shows, read the newspaper, skim through magazines, or listen to the radio. Give them library time to spend browsing through listings of subjects they like in the *Reader's Guide to Periodical Literature*, in a vertical file, or through *Facts on File*.

Learning about topics, questions, and hypotheses

Explain to students the difference between a broad topic, a specific question about the topic, and an hypothesis. This will help the student to narrow the focus and come up with something that will be manageable for an investigation.

A topic, for example, might be "house plants." A specific question might be, "What would happen to house plants if they were watered with sea water rather than fresh water for a period of several weeks?" A hypothesis might be, "I believe that if I watered six different house plants with sea water and six similar plants with fresh water for a period of eight weeks, the plants given fresh water will thrive and the plants watered with salt water will have slowed growth or will die."

Most students can come up with broad topics of interest. With a small amount of help, they can formulate some interesting questions about their topic. The hypothesis might be more difficult for them to write. Remind students that the hypothesis needs to include the subject of the experiment, the variable, and the expected results.

Provide students with class discussion time or a simple work sheet in which they are given several broad topics and asked to come up with questions and hypotheses that might be appropriate for investigation in the school science fair. Emphasize that they need not use any of these items on the work sheet for their own science investigations. But the practice will allow students to gain experience in formulating questions and hypotheses.

Finding information

Once a student has a tentative general topic in mind, and is coming up with some interesting questions, encourage the student to read widely from many sources for information that is available on the topic. There are bibliographies included in this guidebook that might prove useful.

Locating information can be done at home, at school, and at public and some private libraries. Be sure that your students know how to use a card catalogue and a computerized catalogue, and are familiar with the Dewey Decimal System and/or the Library of Congress Classification System. If libraries in your area pool their holdings through a combined database, learn how to use this and explain its use to your students.

Students need to be familiar with both general and specialized encyclopedias. They should consider many possible sources of information including dictionaries, almanacs, yearbooks, biographical sources, and geographical sources. Most students will have used a school or common general encyclopedia. But they might never have heard of such specialized encyclopedias as *ENCYCLO-*

PEDIA OF ANIMAL CARE, McGRAW-HILL ENCYCLOPEDIA OF ENVI-
RONMENTAL SCIENCE, THE WATER ENCYCLOPEDIA, THE NEW
LAROUSE ENCYCLOPEDIA OF THE EARTH, or THE MERCK INDEX:
AN ENCYCLOPEDIA OF CHEMICALS & DRUGS.

Without this knowledge about how to carry out independent research, a student can get lost or badly confused in a large library. As mentioned earlier, your
media specialist is an invaluable resource here.

The teacher needs to explain that if a local library, public or private, does not
have a specific piece of material on hand that a student needs, it might be
found in a branch library. Or the librarian might be willing to request the information for the student through an interlibrary loan. Take some time explaining how this works. This might be an excellent time to invite a public or
private librarian to come into your class as a resource speaker and share such information with students.

From the computerized listing or from the card catalogue, the student should
be taught to look at the copyright date. If the student is doing research on a
current breakthrough, he or she might waste time checking out or ordering
through interlibrary loan a particularly old piece of scholarship on the topic.
Even if it is current, the material might be too difficult or complex for the student to use. Help the student with techniques to glean as much as possible from
the data available before actually ordering or checking out a book.

Magazines might be another excellent source of information for the student.
Students need to be taught how to use *The Reader's Guide to Periodical Literature*
and should be familiar with computerized periodical listings such as *Uncover*.

Experienced teachers should have a variety of documents on hand that they
have gathered by writing to the federal government, state offices, businesses,

and industries. Showing a few pamphlets available through the Department of Energy, the National Aeronautic and Space Administration, the Bureau of Mines, the Fish and Wildlife Service, etc. will allow a student to see firsthand that material is often available simply by sending a written request. For new teachers, there's no time like the present to start building up such a file.

Teachers should also encourage students to seek information through letters and interviews with knowledgeable people in the community or further away. A phone book with subdivisions of governmental agencies might prove to be a valuable resource. It might not occur to students to write to an expert with questions, providing a self-addressed stamped envelope. Not all, but many experts will take the time for a short reply. Students also need to know that, even though they are acquiring information from primary sources, such information should still be credited in their research papers by giving the name of the person interviewed.

If human resources are being consulted, the whole class might benefit from some initial practice. Stage some mock telephone interviews or an in-person interview using student volunteers in which one student pretends to call or meet with a local scientist with questions about a science fair project. Allow other students to critique the interview.

Without practice, students might not realize they need to set an appointment, introduce themselves, and get permission to use a tape recorder if they plan to use one. They also have to prepare the questions in advance, be ready to take notes, and remember to thank the interviewee.

Notes and bibliography cards

At the same time students are researching, they need to take notes and make bibliography cards. Many teachers require the student to hand in these bibliography cards with the finished research paper. Such index cards should include the name of the author, article, book or magazine, the date of publication, a list of the pages consulted, and even some direct quotes that will be used in the paper.

Although the format for bibliographic cards is simple, remember that it might be new to students and parents. Taping an acceptable completed index card to the wall in the classroom so that students might consult it, and photocopying one and including it in informational material that goes home to parents, are good ideas. If the final paper is to contain a bibliography of works consulted, and if you want that to be in a certain format, also give the student a written example of how to indicate quotes in the paper and what a completed bibliography should look like.

Throughout the research process, the student will need to take notes. These notes should be linked back to the bibliographic index cards by a simple system. The bibliographic cards could be numbered, and the numbers should be included on all the notes taken from that source. Or the student might jot down the author's name at the beginning of any notes being taken from that writer's work.

Make the preparation of bibliography cards and note-taking a habit. This can save valuable time by permitting the students to refer back to a source if they later decide to review or quote something from it. Students also need to be taught how to use their notes. They should learn how to quote a brief piece from a book or magazine and to credit the source of the information. They also need to learn how to paraphrase and write information in their own words.

When is enough enough?

Some students get so interested in gathering data that they find it difficult to stop and face actually writing the paper. During class periods devoted to working with students, the teacher can suggest that additional resources are needed or that the student has ample information and needs to begin writing.

The outline

Most elementary students do not thrive on elaborate outlines that include topic, subtopic, undersubtopic, subundersubtopic, and undersubundersubtopic. Such detailed requirements might well sink the paper! When it's required that an outline be turned in with the paper, many honest students will frankly admit that they write the paper first, and then they construct the outline!

There are many organizational approaches, and it's important for the teacher to help the student select one and to construct a simple and fairly broad outline. Encourage students to review the facts they have learned, study their notes, and then try to determine an order of presentation that makes sense.

Should their organizational pattern be chronological, historical, topical, descriptive, or critical? How will the student introduce the main topic, provide a body of information about the topic, tie the various themes together, and come up with a conclusion? Thinking through these questions should provide the outline.

Once the student has a working outline, it will be easy to go back through the notes and bibliographic cards and see where each fits into the broad scheme of the paper. Putting the notes in this order means that the student is now ready to write a rough draft of the paper by hand, or type it, or enter it in a word-processing system.

The teacher might consider providing some class time for student peer editing at this point. One student reads the rough draft of another student. The two students conference together. They ask such questions as: Did the paper get confusing at any point? Are there errors in spelling, punctuation, capitalization, etc.? Were the sources of information credited? Are there unanswered

questions? Such feedback can be very valuable as the student prepares another draft of the paper. The second draft might be reviewed by another student editor, a teacher, a parent, or another interested adult. After this second critique, the student is ready to write and submit the final copy.

Early primary grades

Teachers of early primary students might read all of the preceding background about research papers and think that the science fair is definitely not for them. The age and skill level of many primary-grade students prevent them from carrying out the sorts of processes outlined previously. But that might not mean that the primary student can't participate in the fair.

The school science fair committee is usually ready and willing to tailor some of the "rules and regulations" to fit very young scientists. Perhaps the committee has decided that background research papers are not required for primary-grade students. Maybe a whole class would like to record its questions, guesses, and findings on some chart paper. Perhaps the class will enter a single project in the fair. "What We Learned about Soap Bubbles" might make a fine entry from a kindergarten class.

Sometimes a younger student can work with an older sibling or friend on a topic of mutual interest. Most science fair committees will allow two or three students to work together on a single science fair project. If only a few primary students from a class enter a fair, it is still a great learning opportunity.

The primary-grade teacher might find a time when the exhibits are ready for viewing and take the entire class to the fair. This allows younger students to see what other students have been investigating. This might build an interest in participating themselves when they are older.

Beyond the classroom: Helping with the fair

The conscientious teacher who has motivated students, communicated clearly with students and parents, advised and supported students throughout their investigations, taught them how to keep logs and project notebooks, showed them how to locate resources and find information, explained how to take notes, make an outline, and write their general background paper, might feel that surely now the teacher's job is done. Not so.

There is a great deal to a school science fair that goes beyond the classroom and one group of students. If the fair is to be a success, teachers must be involved in additional ways. Some teachers will serve on the school science fair committee. The final responsibility for the fair rests with this group, but they need all the help they can get! Although teachers have been sending home notes about the fair, the science committee will also need to do some publicity.

The school newsletter should carry information about the fair. Posters might be displayed around the school. A local newspaper might be cajoled into doing an article and including a picture of a student and work in progress. Certificates or ribbons need to be ordered in advance and completed. The gym (or similar room) needs to be reserved well in advance. Special arrangements might have to be made to borrow tables from classrooms or from a central source to have enough platform space to display the projects.

The science fair committee will need to have a set of judges. The committee might well ask each classroom teacher to supply names of parents or community members who might be willing to serve.

The night before, or the morning of the fair, the committee will surely need help in getting each project set up and labeled. Students might be selected to serve as "runners" assigned to each judge. These "runners" can go to classrooms to find and bring participants in the fair to the gym for their judging interview. After the fair, (and yes, there is life after the fair!) more helpers are needed to take down the exhibits and handle the cleanup.

A willingness to help in some aspect of the fair (securing judges, writing publicity, making posters, setting up or taking down exhibits, providing coffee and refreshments for the judges, filling out certificates, etc.) will be of tremendous assistance to the science fair committee. In this function, as well as many others, the old saying is very true: many hands make light work!

And they make for a successful elementary school science fair.

3

The parent's role in the elementary school science fair

Since you are reading this chapter, the chances are very good that your child has decided to do a science project and enter a school science fair. You've been told that your interest and support of this project is really vital to its success. And you're certainly willing to help, but you don't know exactly what is expected of you. This book is designed to help you get started in science fairs.

If you haven't participated in a science fair yourself or recently helped a child with such a project, you might be concerned about how to proceed. Relax and enjoy yourself! With good preplanning, a sense of humor, and plenty of patience, your assistance to your child in this effort can be both fun and satisfying.

Getting familiar with the procedures

Step one is to familiarize yourself with the various procedures associated with this particular science fair. Your child has probably brought home one or more sheets of information about the elementary school science fair. If not, inquire about this. Perhaps the very information you desperately need is tucked in a book in your child's desk or sitting on the floor of a locker at school. If your child professes to "know nothing," make a call to the teacher.

Science fair information booklets contain vital information such as the registration form, a list of various due dates, specifics about the sizes of display boards, the categories in which a project can be entered, etc. In an effort to promote self-reliance, teachers might have supplied students with all of this information but not asked them to take it home for parents to see. Or they might have said it's available on request and haven't had many takers.

Self-reliance is a virtue, but it is one that must be cultivated in the elementary-school-aged student. Unfortunately, it does not spring into full bloom with the announcement of the school science fair. Parents know their children better than anyone. If you suspect that your student will definitely need some help and guidance along the way, request that your child bring home the science fair guidelines.

Once you have read and understood this information, you are in a good position to assist your child. As time progresses, you might find yourself getting very enthusiastic about the project. At the opposite extreme, you might find yourself baffled by the topic. Either way, it's important to keep in mind that this is your child's project, not yours. While you might know a lot, a little, or nothing about the topic under investigation, you can still offer valuable assistance in many ways.

If your child's teacher did not send home parental information, it might be because of experiences in the past where the teacher received the parent's science fair project instead of the child's! You need to guard against such a parental takeover. The actual work must be done by the student.

Asking clarifying questions and providing ongoing interest

Perhaps the next helpful step is to discuss the science fair with your child. Have you or your child ever been to a fair before? Did your child enter a project last year? How did it go? Ask clarifying questions. What sort of project does your child want to enter this year? Why? What is it that your child is trying to demonstrate or learn? What will be the purpose of the investigation?

While you are engaging in discussions of this sort at home, be assured that the classroom teacher is involved in much the same process at school. Many teachers show slides of previous years' science fair projects. They spend time helping students distinguish between general topics, specific questions about a topic, and hypotheses. Such discussions at home and school help the student to clarify thinking and to narrow down a topic to manageable proportions.

Parents need to keep their support of this project in perspective. Every night your first question at the dinner table should not be, "What did you do about your science fair project today?" Constant questioning can cause a child to feel resentful. Nor should you display interest in the project in September and then not mention the subject again until early March. This signals a real lack of interest.

Furnishing supplies and transportation

Once you've held discussions, asked clarifying questions, and know what your child's science fair project will be, as a parent you can continue to be helpful. One function of the parent is to furnish necessary supplies and transportation.

This support is more crucial to the elementary grade student than to the secondary student. Older students might drive a car or easily use public transportation. They might have part-time jobs and have their own money to buy what they need. The elementary grade student is far more dependent upon parents for supplies and transportation.

Your child might need to go to the library to do some reading and research. To carry out an experiment, your son or daughter might need materials that could be located at home or that might need to be ordered or purchased. Art materials, such as magic markers, might be necessary for the science display board. Your child might need access to a computer to prepare a conclusions sheet, to make a graph or table, or even to write a computer program. Perhaps photographs will be included. If so, a camera must be available and time allowed to have prints made for display purposes.

Certainly the secret to success in this area is timing. You need to let your child know that you are willing to help, but that you need to know well in advance when help is needed. If a trip to the library is in order, plan it ahead together and put it on your calendar. If you need to be involved in a shopping trip for science supplies, plan a time for that to happen. If your child needs some home computer time, make sure it isn't the night when big sister needs the computer to finish a term paper.

It's unfair for a child to expect a busy parent or other siblings to drop everything and rearrange their schedules on demand. It's also unfair for a parent to respond to a request for help in the science fair project with a vague, "We'll get to it sometime."

Children as well as their parents are busy people, and all involved in a successful project need to be part of planning ahead. Forming the pattern of setting priorities and planning ahead while working with a science fair project might prove a good model for many other future family activities.

Helping locate resources

To adults, some things look obvious. These same things might not be at all obvious to the elementary school student. It should also be recognized that because of prior experience, or the lack of it, children of the same age and grade also vary widely in life experiences. They also differ in personalities and their approach to activities.

The child who is outgoing and talkative and who has had easy access to the telephone at home might feel quite comfortable in calling up a number of nurseries to ask questions about plants and fertilizers. Another child might be a good deal more comfortable talking to someone in person. Still another might prefer to do a lot of reading. Parents are in an excellent position to thoroughly know their child and to be supportive of those approaches that will best enable the student to succeed.

If the teacher is devoting class time to helping students learn how to acquire government pamphlets, explaining about various libraries in the area that might be helpful, and discussing how to find experts in various fields, your child might have a good idea of where to begin. The parent's role can be to help the student follow up on these leads. If sufficient assistance is not being given in the classroom, as an interested parent, you might need to take the initiative here.

Serving as a resource person in an area of expertise

If you've heeded the warning about not exerting undue influence on your child in the selection of a topic and not taking over the science fair project as "yours," you might find yourself in an interesting situation. You might be an expert in mechanical engineering and know almost nothing about an area of botany where your child is carrying out an investigation.

In many ways, this is a great position to be in. If you aren't an expert in the field, there is far less possibility of your unduly influencing the flow of the project. You and your young scientist will make discoveries together that might surprise you both.

But the expertise that you have is very valuable. Be alert to requests in a teacher's letter or in the school's newsletter to volunteer additional help if you have time. Perhaps on the day of the fair you could serve as a judge for the projects that are entered in the engineering category. Perhaps there's a student working on an engineering project who would really benefit from talking over a problem with you. If you have time, volunteer your services. They'll probably be snapped up!

Serving as a mentor for a student working on a project can be very rewarding. It can also be time-consuming. Before launching into a mentorship, be sure that you have the time to see it through.

As in the case of helping your own child, you must be careful in a mentoring position to simply support the student and not to take over the project. And even though the project for which you are serving as a mentor might be very different from your child's science fair project, you might gain some additional insights into the process and procedures associated with the fair, and these might prove helpful in your parenting role.

Providing a suitable and safe work space

No matter how big or small the house or apartment, it never seems adequate in terms of space for the science fair project. Space certainly has to be a consideration early on, even in selecting the specific project. If the student is going to have to set up 20 fish tanks, where will the fish tanks go? If the seedlings need sunshine, where will the flower pots sit? Assuming that the project needs are within the realm of possibility, some ground rules might need to be set.

A family conference might be a good way to discuss the science fair investigation. Siblings need to be made aware of the fact that this is serious study. They must learn to respect the project. The student who is carrying out the investigation also needs to keep things neat, put materials in their place, and be responsible.

You can't be too safety conscious with a science fair project. Help your young scientist consider all the safety factors involved. Remember that anything that is really hazardous will be prohibited at the fair. For example, the science fair committee will probably state that open flames cannot be used at the fair.

Some things might seem safe that really aren't. For example, when mixed, many chemicals (including some household cleansers) can be dangerous. If electricity is involved, be sure that extension cords are in good shape and that a three-pronged grounded plug is used. If glassware is going to be heated, be certain that it is able to withstand the temperatures involved.

Being a cheerleader

Once the science investigation is well under way, your job, as parent, is primarily to serve as a cheerleader. At this point, the topic has been selected for research, an hypothesis has been formulated, and the experimentation is taking place.

But even if all has been going well so far, your child might have a tendency to slack off at some point. While leaving for baseball practice, the young scientist might call over his shoulder, "Water my plants for me, will you, Mom?" Or, "Will you finish entering my bibliography into the computer, Dad?"

As a parent, it is easy to get pulled into doing the project instead of being your child's cheerleader. Guard against this. A science fair project can take several months. Be sure that your child plans ahead, makes time for the important things to be done, and carries out responsibilities.

Also be aware that sometimes everything goes wrong! Then the cheerleading is tough. Sometimes, due to a fluke such as a power failure while all of you were out of town visiting relatives, a part of the science fair experiment is ruined. The child must begin anew. This can be disheartening.

Perhaps it becomes clear that the hypothesis that was so carefully formulated by the child is quite wrong. Help your student understand that it is valuable to conduct an experiment and find out through a series of careful observations that although the hypothesis looked promising, it was incorrect.

A word about the background research paper

Some teachers will require a background research paper, a project log, and/or project notebook along with the actual science fair project to be put on display. If the teacher has provided checkpoints along the way when a tentative topic, a preliminary bibliography, and a rough draft of the paper have been due, your young scientist might be right on target.

If there have not been checkpoints, your child might have done a great project but not have done any of the required writing to accompany it. When you are clarifying policies and procedures of the fair, as mentioned previously, be sure that you also learn about any written requirements. Knowing what these are, you can help your son or daughter devote time to this aspect of the fair. Sometimes a teacher is blamed for "dumping" a huge assignment on students when, in reality, all were informed of due dates well in advance.

At last—Going to the fair!

After all this time and effort has been expended, both at home and at school, it might go without saying that you should try hard to visit the fair. Remember that your child might be a perfectionist who feels that his or her project "didn't turn out as well as it should have." Or he or she might be under the impression that, "Everyone else did something more interesting and exciting than I did." So perhaps out of a sense of inadequacy or embarrassment, your presence might not have been demanded at the fair.

Try to go anyway. Give honest and positive feedback to your child and to other students that you might meet at the fair. If no one attended an orchestra concert or no one came to the basketball tournament, the participants and the sponsors would be disappointed. This is true of the elementary school science fair, too.

In addition to supporting your child and other students, try to locate the school administrator and some of the teachers at the fair and express your appreciation to them. You might have suggestions for improvement, and these should certainly be offered in a positive and respectful way in the near future. But on the night of the fair, accentuate the positive! It should be the happy culmination of a lot of hard work!

4
The scientific method

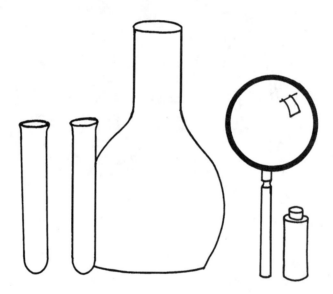

Whatever type of science fair project students choose, (see chapter 5), they will want to follow some sort of method throughout the investigation. While some people believe there is "one scientific method" that scientists always follow, this is not the case. Each scientific problem has certain conditions that dictate a portion of the method that is appropriate to be used.

One common "scientific method" that is often employed in carrying out science fair investigations has six basic steps: purpose, hypothesis, procedure, data gathering, results, and conclusions. It might prove useful to elementary students to consider each of these steps as they move through a science fair investigation.

Purpose

The purpose of a science fair project is usually stated as a question to be answered. Such preliminary questions can be formulated regardless of what type of project is going to be carried out. For example, the student who is doing a comparative survey might ask, "Is left-handedness more common in boys than in girls?" For an investigation about magnetism, a question might be posed in this way: "When a wire is attached to a battery to form a magnet, is there a relationship between the number of coils of the wire wrapped around an iron core and the strength of the magnet?"

Before scientists undertake an investigation, they usually do a lot of reading in their field. This is sometimes referred to as background research or making "reference to authority." It simply means that the scientist tries to find out what has already been done that relates to the problems currently under investigation. There are many scientific journals, books, and general magazines that publish the results of scientific research. Scientists try to keep current in their reading.

Hypothesis

The hypothesis that the young scientist formulates and sets out to prove through a science fair investigation might be considered an educated guess in answer to the beginning question. It is formulated after the student has done some of the initial thinking and reading discussed previously, but before a thorough investigation is carried out.

An hypothesis might be based on some initial observations. These observations could be made through the senses of sight, smell, touch, hearing, and taste. They might also involve the use of scientific instruments such as microscopes or telescopes.

The hypothesis posed for the science fair project should be written in one sentence, and it needs to state the subject of the experiment, the variable that will be changed or measured, and the results that the student expects. The following are examples. In a comparative survey, the following hypothesis might be tested: the pulse rate in fifth graders listening to a classical waltz for ten minutes will be 25% lower than the pulse rate of those listening to a rock-and-roll selection of music for the same length of time because rock-and-roll music is louder and faster.

In an investigation, the hypothesis might be: sea water will retard the growth in chrysanthemums, philodendrons, and marigolds due to the high salt content, which is toxic to plants. And a hypothesis posed around questions raised when considering a rock collection might be: the broken surfaces inside river rocks will be rougher than their outside surfaces because sand and water have smoothed off the outer surface of the river rocks.

Procedure

The procedure for carrying out a science fair project is a logical extension of the initial reading and observation that went into formulating the hypothesis. It will probably fall into two categories. The first is more research. Although a good deal of reading might already have taken place, the student will want to read more information from books, newspapers, magazines, pamphlets, etc. on the selected topic.

Information can also be gathered from observations and from talking to experts, watching a television show, or visiting an exhibit. This research is also an important component of the background research paper, which is often required to be turned in with the completed science fair project. Then there will be experimentation, which involves more observation and might include some trial and error, in which the student tests the hypothesis.

Gathering the data

For example, a student could hypothesize that using a specific computer program for half an hour would improve fifth graders' scores on a division test more than spending half an hour on a written work sheet because of the more exciting visual game format of the computer program. The young scientist will then set out to prove this.

The teacher might agree to arrange for a class to take a division test one day. The next day, half of the students would spend 30 minutes on a division work sheet while half spend 30 minutes on a computer program involving division in a game format. Then the teacher would retest, and the science student would compare the results of the two groups.

During some experiments, there will be variables, controls, and experimental and control groups. Care must be taken not to confuse these or to be careless; otherwise the results of the investigation will be worthless. For example, a student makes the hypothesis that the leaves of ivy plants deprived of sunlight for a month will turn pale and die, while those exposed to sunlight will thrive. The only variable in the hypothesis in the amount of light that the two groups of plants will receive each day. But if the student puts one group of ivy plants in a closet to be certain that they don't receive sunlight, and also forgets to give them any water, another variable has been included in the experiment.

It's important during experimentation for students to keep up with writing in the project log and notebook discussed in detail in chapter 1. Students should make an entry in the log whenever they work on the project and note observations at the same time each day. When students get into a regular routine, they won't have to "guess" what day it was that the seed first sent a shoot up above the ground or how tall a seedling was two days ago.

To have reliable data, students must include several repetitions. If, for example, the student needs to know how long it takes for a 1-inch cube of ice to melt in a glass of 65-degree Fahrenheit tap water, the student should repeat this procedure for several trials, and time each trial. Then the experimenter can take an average that should be reliable. And, if there are wide variations in the trials, the experimenter needs to look at the possible cause of the variation.

Results

After the experimentation and gathering of data is complete, the results need to be listed. This often involves using a variety of math skills since these results can be written out and/or shown in charts or graphs. In some cases photographs might be used to show "before and after" or "comparison" results. It is important that the results be clearly stated. They should represent facts rather than opinions. (A fact is something that has been proved to be true. An opinion is something that you believe to be true.)

In working with results, students also need to give careful thought to sources of error. If in the ice-melting times listed previously, one of the recorded melting times is greatly different from all the others, could the student have misread the time? Did the investigator reverse figures when recording the time? Scientific investigators continue to try to eliminate as many errors as possible.

Conclusions

Once all the data is gathered and studied, the experimenter looks back at the hypothesis to see whether it was proved true or false. If the project was not an investigation, but was rather the construction of a model or display of a collection, the conclusion might discuss the questions that were raised, suggest what the project might lead to, or consider what is its importance.

It is also wise to be cautious with conclusions. A student might have come up with a conclusion based on a procedure involving measuring the effect of one variable. Perhaps other variables were involved that the student did not consider. Perhaps the sample size that was used was not large enough, and if the sample size was doubled, would have revealed quite a different result. A student might have made an error in the materials used. For example, perhaps the flour that was added to a mixture contained salt. If the student discovers or suspects some problem in the procedure that might have affected the results of the project, this should be included in the write-up of the project.

List the steps for clarity

If the young scientist follows these six steps and lists them on the science fair display board, it will help the viewer see the purpose of the project, the hypothesis that was formulated, the procedures used to gather data to support the hypothesis, and the results and conclusions that were drawn.

5
Types of projects

There are many types of projects that are accepted at the elementary school science fair. Several types are discussed in this chapter.

Investigations

Science fair investigations can take any one of three different forms: comparative surveys, controlled experiments, and simple experiments. *Comparative surveys* are sometimes called "natural experiments." A survey is a useful approach for the student who identifies two or more groups that might be alike in many ways but might show a difference in one or more factors. For example, a student might want to compare the differences between the heartbeats of boys and girls. The hypothesis might be that while sitting at rest in the classroom, fifth-grade boys' hearts beat faster than the hearts of fifth-grade girls.

A *controlled experiment* would be used for a project where a student worked with an experimental group, a control group, and a variable. An example of this type of experiment might be keeping all other conditions the same but watering almost identical plants using sea water for the experimental group of plants and fresh water for the control group of plants. The experimenter would then observe any difference that the variable made in plant growth.

The purpose of a *simple experiment* is to show a change in something. For example, a student might fasten a balloon to the top of a plastic soda bottle filled with cola, and then, with a string, measure the diameter of the balloon after one, two, and three minutes have passed. In this way, the investigator would be able to show that the balloon was being inflated by the release of carbon dioxide gas from the cola.

Demonstrations

Rather than carry out an investigation like those just described, a student might choose to do a demonstration. Such a demonstration could take one of three forms: demonstrating a scientific principle, demonstrating a complex natural phenomenon, or demonstrating how a practical product of some sort works.

A student wanting to *demonstrate a scientific principle* might, for example, show how Ohm's law works. Making a cloud chamber would be an example of demonstrating a *complex natural phenomenon*. Building a model of the Panama Canal to demonstrate how locks work or writing a computer program to run a robot would be examples of a *demonstration of a practical product*.

Collections

A third type of elementary school science fair project that a student might consider would be to prepare a collection for display. A student might, for example, display a rock collection or make a display of different types of insulation materials and their uses.

As pointed out earlier, simply gathering a collection of materials or making a model is not sufficient in and of itself as a science fair project. A good science fair project requires that the student take some additional steps besides bringing in a collection.

For example, the student who wants to display a collection of rocks might ask some interesting questions about rocks, such as: Do all rocks have the same hardness? Does the density of a rock correlate with its hardness? Then the student can make a hypothesis and test it by using the rocks in the rock collection.

If a student makes a model of a ship, that student needs to go on and ask some questions about the shape of ships, the displacement of water, what makes things sink or float, etc. in order to have a good science fair project. Then the student can make an hypothesis and carry out an investigation using the ship model to answer the questions that are raised. When carrying out any one of these types of science fair investigations, a student should follow the scientific method, which is discussed in detail in chapter 4.

6
Possible projects in botany

A science fair project in botany can be particularly satisfying. One important thing to remember is that many projects in this area can't be done hastily. Time is required to show the differences that variables make in plant growth. Time is also needed for seeds, flowering plants, and vegetables to grow and reach maturity.

As in other categories, you might plan an experiment, carry out a survey, or bring in a collection to help answer some scientific questions. In the examples that follow, you will be presented with a number of ideas. Just reading them over might suggest interesting variations so that you can make the project uniquely your own. So plan an exciting botany project and get started early!

One of the simplest projects might be to hypothesize about whether or not the depth that seeds are planted will make a difference in their growth. From what was discussed in chapter 4, remember that you should approach your project using a six-step method.

Experiment 1:
The effect of depth of soil on seed growth
Category: Botany, grades K–5

Materials needed: Large, clear plastic or glass container(s); gravel; potting soil; 25 radish seeds; black construction paper; rubber band or tape; science log or notebook.

1. The purpose of your experiment is to answer the question, "Does it make a difference how deep you plant seeds?"
2. The hypothesis. If five radish seeds are planted at five different depths in the soil, but otherwise treated in the same way, the seed planted the shallowest will be the tallest plant in six weeks.
3. The procedure. To carry out your experiment, you will need a large, clear plastic or glass container. (An old aquarium will do nicely.) Or you can use five wide-mouthed jars.

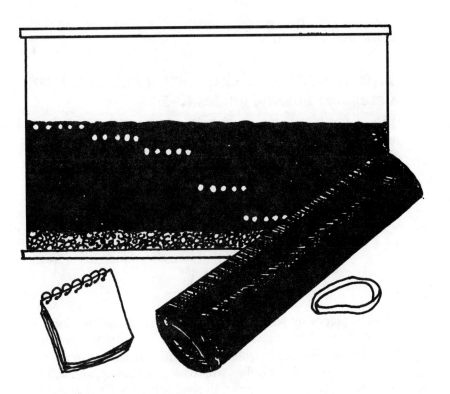

- Put a layer of gravel at the bottom of the aquarium or the five jars to assure good drainage. Then add about 6 inches of good potting soil. Soak radish seeds overnight to loosen the seed coat.
- Next, plant the radish seeds at different depths in the large container or in the five jars. Plant five seeds near the top of the soil, five seeds 1 inch deep, five seeds 2 inches deep, five seeds 4 inches deep, and five seeds 5 inches deep.
- Plant the seeds next to the outside wall of your container(s) so that you will be able to observe growth.
- Cover the sides of the jars or the aquarium with black construction paper so that sunlight does not shine on the seeds. Use a rubber band or tape to keep the black paper in place.

4. Data gathering. Once each day, remove the paper and observe your seeds. Record what you see in your log or notebook. If you notice no change, be sure to record that, too. Water your seeds carefully and keep the soil moist, but not wet. Continue to do this for six weeks.

5. The results. After six weeks of equal care, what results do you have? Are plants consistently healthier looking or taller from the seeds planted at a certain depth? Did some seeds never sprout? Are the results inconsistent?

6. The conclusion. Using these results, what can you say about your hypothesis? Was it correct or incorrect? Were the shallowest-planted radish seeds the tallest plants in six weeks?

Plants can be grown in various mediums. First you might want to do a little reading as background research. What generally is said about different kinds of soil and plant growth? Once you have some basic information, you might want

Experiment 1: The effect of depth of soil on seed growth

to carry out an experiment to determine which medium would be best for a particular plant's growth.

Experiment 2: Using different plant mediums
Category: Botany, grades K–5

Materials needed: Five small flowering plants in pots (such as marigolds), vermiculite, garden soil, potting soil, sand, science log or notebook.

1. The purpose of your experiment is to answer the question, "Which medium is best to promote the growth of a specific flowering plant?"
2. The hypothesis. Marigolds of the same size, treated in the same way, will be healthier plants (fuller, with dark green leaves, and will produce more and larger flowers) if grown in good potting soil rather than in some other medium for two months.
3. The procedure. Purchase five of the same kind of flowering plants (marigolds or others of your choice) that are nearly identical in size.
   - At home, remove one of the plants from its pot. Gently rinse and remove as much soil as possible from the roots. Repot this plant right back in the soil it came in. (It's important to do this because this will be your "control," and you need to be sure that you have "disturbed" its growth by digging it up just as you will disturb the other plants in your experiment.)
   - With the other four plants, remove each one from its pot and gently rinse and remove the original soil. Then replant each plant. Plant one in sand, one in vermiculite, one in topsoil from your backyard, and one in good potting soil.
   - Use the same watering schedule for each of your five plants. Put all the plants in the same area so that they will get the same amount of sunlight and are kept at the same temperature.
4. Data gathering. Carefully chart and log what you see after one week, two weeks, etc. Continue this for eight weeks.
5. The results. Examine your plants to answer the following questions: Which plant is fullest? Which is tallest? What color are the leaves of each of the plants? Which has the best and most blossoms?
6. The conclusion. Was your hypothesis correct? Was the plant in your good potting soil the healthiest-looking plant after eight weeks? (It was fuller, taller, had more and brighter flowers, and had dark green leaves.)

Vegetables are an important part of our diet. Some people are able to plant home gardens and supply themselves with fresh vegetables. Just like farmers, these backyard gardeners need to decide when to pick or pull their crops.

How do backyard gardeners know when to pull up or pick their vegetables? You might want to do a little background research first. Remember that you could read about vegetable gardening in books and magazines and that you might conduct some in-person interviews with gardeners. You might try the following experiment with beets to decide if leaf size is a good indicator of the size of the beet in the ground.

Experiment 3: What does leaf size indicate?
Category: Botany, grades 4–5

Materials needed: Beet seeds, garden plot or planting container, tape measure, science log or notebook.

1. The purpose of your experiment is to answer the question, "Is leaf size a good indicator of the size of the beet in the ground?"
2. The hypothesis. Plants with the most and largest leaves will have the largest beets.

3. The procedure. Plant beet seeds in a container or in a small patch of your garden. Water and tend them carefully and be sure that they receive plenty of sunlight.

4. Data gathering. After they have had a chance to grow to maturity, pull two beets. Pick two plants that you think have about the same size/amount of leaves. In your notebook or science log, enter the date you pulled the beets.
   • Measure the length and circumference of the edible part of the beet. Add the two lengths together and divide by two to get an average length. Add the two circumferences together and divide by two to get the average circumference. Then measure the length and width of each leaf. Multiply and add together all the products to get a total for each plant. Then add the two totals together and divide by two to get a rough average of the leaf surfaces of the pair of plants.
   • Repeat this process every seven days for a full month.

5. The results. As the plants grew longer, the leaves probably got bigger. Chart the data that you collected over a month. Then evaluate your data.

6. The conclusion. Was your hypothesis correct? Do beets with more leaf surface have bigger roots?

Seeds of plants are great weight lifters. You might have noticed this if you've planted seeds at home and watched them grow. Sometimes the seed will break through the ground and begin growing with a chunk of dried dirt still stuck to it, showing where it broke through the soil. You can do a science fair experiment on weight lifters.

Experiment 4: Popcorn seeds can lift weight
Category: Botany, grades K–5

Materials needed: Popcorn, plastic glass, small plastic plate, science log or notebook.

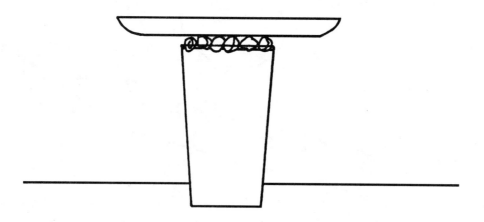

1. The purpose of your experiment is to answer the question, "Do different kinds of dried seeds have the ability to lift an object such as a plastic plate that is set over them?"

2. The hypothesis. If dried popcorn is put in a plastic glass and water is added so that it is up to the rim of the glass, and a small plastic plate is put on top, the "weight-lifting" seeds will push the plate off.

3. The procedure. Fill a clear plastic glass with raw kernels of popcorn. Put it in the center of a table. Then add water right up to the rim of the glass. Cover the top of the glass with a small, plastic plate.

4. Data gathering. Check the plastic glass every hour. In your log or science notebook, write down what you see. Before long, you should see the plate rise above the rim of the glass. Leave the popcorn there overnight. Check it again in the morning.

5. The results. In the morning, you will probably find that the plastic plate has fallen over onto the table. It has been pushed away by the dry kernels of popcorn absorbing water and swelling up.

6. The conclusion. Was your hypothesis correct? Did the weight-lifting seeds manage to lift the plastic plate right off of them?

Many people are fascinated by plant seeds. They come in many shapes and sizes and have special ways of traveling. You might decide to enter a seed collection in the science fair. Remember, if you do this your entry will be a much better one if you go beyond just labeling the seeds on a display board.

Try to think of some interesting questions that you might be able to answer using what you have learned while making your seed collection. One of the things that you might have learned is that seeds need air to spout.

Experiment 5: Seeds need air to sprout
Category: Botany, grades 3–5

Materials needed: Two glass jars, one with a tight lid; two jars of pea seeds; your science log or notebook.

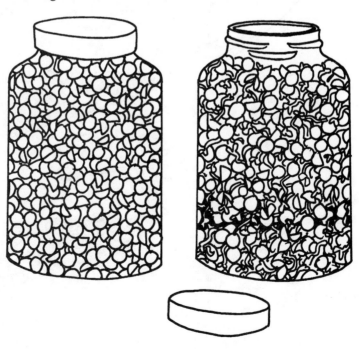

1. The purpose of your experiment is to answer the question, "Do seeds need air in order to sprout?"

2. The hypothesis. If two identical jars of peas with water are kept side by side, and one is open to the air while the other is sealed to keep air out, the peas in the open jar will sprout while the ones in the tightly closed jar will not sprout.

3. The procedure. Fill two jars with peas. Add a small amount of water to each. Shake the jars to moisten the seeds. Tightly seal one jar with a lid. Leave the other jar open. Put the jars side by side in a sunny window. As water evaporates from the open jar, add a little more to keep the peas moist.

4. Data gathering. Each day observe the two jars. In your science log or notebook, record what you see.

5. The results. Seeds in one jar sprouted while seeds in the second jar did not.

6. The conclusion. Was your hypothesis correct? Were you able to prove that seeds need air in order to sprout?

Here's another question you might investigate in connection with a seed collection using the same materials that you had in experiment 5.

Experiment 6:
Seeds take oxygen from the air
Category: Botany, grades 3–5

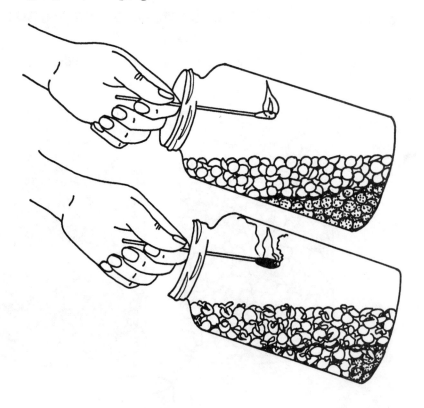

1. The purpose of your experiment is to answer the question, do sprouting seeds use up oxygen?
2. The hypothesis. Sprouting seeds will use up the oxygen in a jar as they grow.
3. The procedure. Use the jar of sprouting seeds from experiment 5. Put them in a glass jar with a half inch of water in the bottom. In another jar of the same size, add the same amount of unsprouted, dry peas. Cover both jars tightly.
4. Data gathering. Wait a full day and then perform your oxygen test. Loosen the top of the jar with the dried peas. Strike a match. Remove the lid and hold the match in the jar. Loosen the top of the jar with the sprouting peas. Strike a match. Remove the lid and quickly put the match into the jar. Note your observations in your science log or notebook.
5. The results. One of the matches will continue to burn while the other one goes out because there is not sufficient oxygen to support the flame.
6. The conclusion. Was your hypothesis correct? Did you prove that sprouting seeds use up oxygen?

Lots of people love to eat peanuts. Often they buy their nuts in a can or jar from the store. These nuts are shelled and salted. Sometimes people buy peanuts in shells, but theses have been roasted. For this next experiment, you will need raw peanuts.

When you raise a plant at home, you usually put it in a sunny spot where it gets light. Some plants like lots of sunshine, and others like partial shade, but they all need light to grow. Have you ever wondered what would happen if you could increase the amount of light that your plants get? Would they grow faster?

Experiment 7: Using light at night for plants
Category: Botany, grades K–5.

Materials needed: Fluorescent light, raw peanuts, two pots, potting soil, baking pan, plastic wrap, science log or notebook.

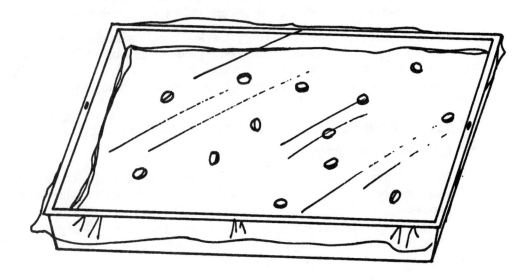

1. The purpose of your experiment is to answer the question, "If I increased the amount of light that one pot of plants received and did not increase the amount of light that another identical pot of plants received, would the plants with the extra light grow more?"

2. The hypothesis. If I kept a fluorescent light on all night above one pot of peanut plants, and did not light another pot of peanut plants, and if both plants were kept side by side during the day and watered the same amount, the peanut plants that were under the light at night would grow faster than the plants in the other pot.

3. The procedure. Take raw peanuts and put them in a shallow baking pan on top of several layers of paper towels. Wet the paper towels thoroughly. Cover the baking pan with clear plastic wrap.

    • After the seeds swell and the skins break, wait until seedlings grow. Roots will push from one end, and stems will sprout from the other end. Be sure to keep the paper towels wet so the seedlings will not dry out. When they are big enough, plant six seedlings in a pot of planting soil. Plant another six seedlings in an identical pot of planting soil.

    • Put the two pots with your tiny peanut plants in a sunny window. Water and tend them until they are growing into healthy little plants.

    • Take one pot of plants and set it under a fluorescent light every night. During the day, set both pots of plants next to one another in the sunny window.

4. Data gathering. Measure all of the plants and record their height and the number of leaves each plant has. Enter in your log the time that you put one pot under the fluorescent light every night. Each morning, measure each of the plants again. Continue this procedure for a month. Be sure to keep the soil in both pots moist.

5. The results. After a month, you should be able to see the results from one pot of plants receiving more light than the other. One pot of plants should be taller and bigger than the plants in the pot that never receives light at night.

6. The conclusion. Did you prove your hypothesis? Using identical seedlings, with all conditions the same except for the fact that one group was placed under a fluorescent lamp at night, did the group of plants that received the extra light grow bigger and taller than the other plants?

Here's another experiment involving plants and light. You might notice when you shop for plants that some are described as needing "full sun," while others are listed as doing best in "partial shade." Although all plants have different needs, they do need some light and will seek it even under difficult circumstances.

Experiment 8: Will plants seek the light?
Category: Botany, grades 3–6

Materials needed: You will need an empty margarine or cottage cheese tub, three navy beans, a shoe box with a lid, some potting soil, your science log or notebook.

1. The purpose of your experiment is to answer the question, "Will plants seek the light even if they have to grow sideways to find it?"

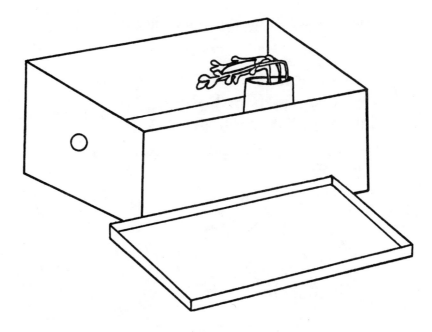

2. The hypothesis. When they cannot grow straight up to find the light, bean seedlings will grow sideways to find the light.

3. The procedure. Soak three navy beans overnight to soften the outside. The next day, plant the three in a small tub of good potting soil. Water them. Take a shoe box, and in the middle of one end, cut out a circle with a 1½ inch diameter. Put the plastic container with the bean seeds into the shoe box at the opposite end from where you have cut the hole. Put on the shoe box lid. Put your box in a sunny window. Open the box now and then to water the seeds.

4. Data gathering. Each day, briefly open the box to water your seeds if they need it, and note what you see. Record the data in your science log or notebook.

5. The results. You will find that the seedlings will grow sideways to find the light and will head out the opening of the shoe box.

6. The conclusion. Was your hypothesis correct? Did all the seedlings grow sideways and seek the light?

Linnaeus was a famous scientist who is said to have made a flower clock. He carefully studied a number of different flowering plants and learned that some of them have blossoms that open and close at the same time each day. By knowing which blossoms open and close at which times, Linnaeus could guess the time by looking at the flowers in his garden.

There is a flower called the four-o'clock, for example, that opens its blossoms around four in the afternoon. As they are opening, other flowers, like the California poppy, are closing.

You will want to do some background reading and to talk with some gardeners before you do your "time-telling" experiment. You'll learn that you cannot really make an accurate clock using flowers because many things affect the time at which blossoms open and close. Some of these factors are: whether it is a sunny or cloudy day, the latitude at which you live, daylight-savings time, temperature, etc.

Experiment 9:
Does warmth or light make a tulip open?
Category: Botany, grades 3–5

Materials needed: Six freshly cut tulips, three tall clear glasses, science log or notebook.

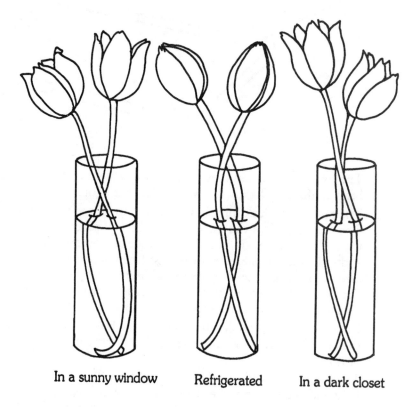

In a sunny window   Refrigerated   In a dark closet

1. The purpose of your experiment is to answer the question, "Do tulips open because of light or because of warmth?"
2. The hypothesis. Tulips open when it is warm, whether or not it is light.
3. The procedure. Get six freshly cut tulips. Put them in a jar of water and place them in the refrigerator for an hour. After an hour, leave two of the tulips in the water in the refrigerator. Take two of the tulips and put them in water at room temperature and put them in a sunny, warm window. Take two tulips and put them in a jar of water at room temperature and put them in a dark closet that is warm.
4. Data gathering. Check on all six tulips every fifteen minutes. In your log or science notebook, write what you observe. You might want to include sketches of what you observe.
5. The results. You will notice that the tulips in the refrigerator remain closed. The tulips in the dark and the tulips in the light both open in the warmth.

6. The conclusion. Was your hypothesis correct? Did you prove that it is warmth and not light that causes the tulip flowers to open?

Most people enjoy eating lovely, ripe fruit. But often the fruit that you buy at the grocery store is "green" and needs time to ripen. What are the factors that affect ripening?

If you do some background reading you will learn that ripening fruit takes up oxygen and gives off carbon dioxide. The oxygen is needed for the chemical reaction involved in ripening. Ripening fruit also gives off ethylene. The ethylene stimulates more ripening.

Experiment 10: Ripening bananas
Category: Botany, grades 3–6

Materials needed: One ripe banana, six green bananas, two paper bags, one plastic bag, science log or notebook.

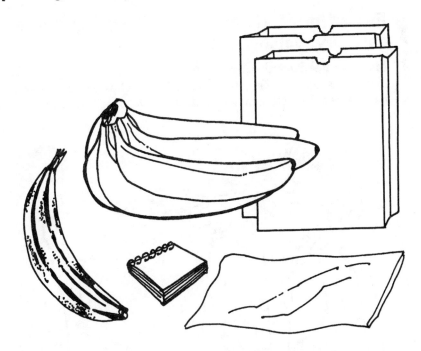

1. The purpose of your experiment is to answer the question, "Can you slow down the process of ripening bananas?"
2. The hypothesis. Green bananas placed in a plastic bag will ripen more slowly than bananas in paper bags or green bananas placed near other ripe fruit.
3. The procedure. Buy six very green bananas and one very ripe banana. Put two green bananas in a paper bag and fold over the top securely several times to seal out the air. Put one green banana and the ripe banana in another paper bag and fold over the top securely several times. Put two green bananas in a plastic bag and use a twist tie to seal the bag tightly. Leave one green banana out on a kitchen counter exposed to air.

4. Data gathering. Wait five days and then open the bags and inspect all seven of the bananas. Note which fruit is still green, which is yellow, and which is brown.

5. The results. The green bananas in the paper bag ripen more quickly than the green bananas in the plastic bag. The green banana with the ripe banana in the paper bag ripens more quickly than the two green bananas in the paper bag. The banana left on the counter turns brown most quickly, and the side touching the counter ripens more quickly than the other side.

6. Conclusion. Was your hypothesis correct? Can you change factors to slow down the ripening of bananas by limiting their exposure to oxygen and to ethylene?

Although you might not realize it, the sense of smell is important to what you taste. You can conduct a survey of taste/smell with a group of your friends to prove this.

 # Experiment 11: How smell affects taste
Category: Botany, grades 3–5

 Materials needed: Two peeled raw apples, two peeled raw potatoes, two peeled raw onions, three paper plates, blindfold, nose clips, grater, three plastic forks, a basin, sheet that lists names of all the subjects, pencil, science log or notebook.

1. The purpose of your experiment is to answer the question, "Can using their sense of smell help people distinguish between raw apples, potatoes, and onions?"

2. The hypothesis. More mistakes will be made by people in the survey when they try to distinguish between the tastes of raw apples, potatoes, and onions without using their sense of smell.

3. The procedure. Find a dozen friends who are willing to take part in your taste/smell experiment. Use a fine grater to grate the raw potato, onion, and apple onto separate paper plates. Be sure to wash the grater very thoroughly after each use. Blindfold a friend and put on the nose clips.
   - Use a plastic fork to put about ¼ teaspoon of the food on the subject's tongue. Tell the subject not to chew the food but to roll it around in the mouth and then to spit it out in a basin. The subject tells you what kind of food it was. Then the subject rinses out the mouth before trying a second sample. Use a separate fork for each kind of food and wash it after every use.
   - Repeat the preceding process, but this time do not use nose clips.

4. Data gathering. You will need to prepare two sheets ahead of time, one labeled "With nose clips" and one labeled "Without nose clips." On each sheet, write the subjects names down the left side and rule off six columns across the top, headed: apple, apple, onion, onion, potato, potato. As each subject tastes a bit of apple, enter in that column what the subject thought the food was. Under apple, for example, you might enter "P" for a guess that it was potato. When you offer the apple again, the subject might guess "O" this time, for onion. Enter it in the second column under apple. Present the samples in random order, but be sure you know what food item is being sampled and be sure to offer each food twice to each subject who is wearing the nose clip. Then repeat the process and offer each food twice to each subject while the subject is not wearing the nose clip.

5. The results. You have a lot of data and can examine it in a variety of ways. How many subjects were right in all six taste tests? How many made mistakes? What percentage of subjects made at least one mistake? Did your subjects name the food more accurately the first or second time they tasted it? Did that make any difference? Was there a difference between the abilities of boys and girls to discriminate? Most importantly, were more mistakes made when the nose clips were used?

6. The conclusion. Was your hypothesis correct? Did your subjects make more mistakes when they tried to identify the three foods without being able to use their sense of smell?

Other possible topics for investigation in botany

➤ Compare the dehydration rate in three different types of sliced apples.

➤ Study the effects of different amounts of water on plant growth.

➤ Study the effects of different amounts of sunlight on plant growth.

➤ Set up two small aquaria. Establish water plants in both. Then bubble carbon dioxide through one of the tanks and not the other. Do this every few days for a month. What happens to plant growth?

➤ Experiment with pine cones to see how much heat is required for the cone to release its seeds.

➤ Devise an experiment to show how water circulates through plants.

➤ Gather and identify as many air-carried seeds as possible. Label them.

➤ Gather and identify seeds that are not airborne. Label them. By what different means do these seeds travel?

➤ Lichens are made up of fungi and algae. Without one, the other dies. Experiment to show how lichens react to various types of air pollution.

➤ Devise an experiment to show transpiration in plants.

➤ Partly uncover a growing carrot and expose the top to air as a demonstration of photosynthesis.

➤ Is one temperature better for the growth of one type of seed while another temperature is best for a different kind of seed?

➤ Seeds germinate faster if they are soaked in water before planting. Does the length of time they are soaked make a difference in how long it takes them to sprout? What would happen if you soaked them in tea, coffee, or lemon juice?

➤ Use a water test kit and test the leachate from soils for the presence of nitrate and phosphate.

➤ Do hydroponic plants that grow in a liquid nutrient solution require less roots than terrestrial plants?

➤ If seeds are frozen, will they still germinate?

➤ If you cover one or more leaves on a plant, what will happen to the leaf and to the plant?

➤ Is incandescent light better than fluorescent light for growing plants?

➤ If you are using a light for your plant growth, can it be on 24 hours a day, or do plants do better if there is a period of time without light in each 24-hour cycle?

➤ How does an oil spill affect plant life? What would happen if you added cooking oil or light motor oil in small quantities to a potted plant?

➤ Design an experiment to show that a plant will grow toward the light (phototropism.)

➤ Show the different ways in which mushrooms reproduce. Make some spore prints.

➤ Demonstrate the "greenhouse effect" by using two large jars (one open and one closed), sunlight, and two thermometers.

➤ Where do plants store starch—in the leaf, stem, or root?

➤ Does photosynthesis take place when it is dark?

➤ What will happen to a plant if you coat the underside of its leave with petroleum jelly so that it cannot "breathe?"

➤ What effect does compacted soil have on plants?

➤ Show different ways of growing plants by using seeds to start some plants and using cuttings to start others.

➤ Devise an experiment to show that because seedlings have no chlorophyll, they cannot give off oxygen as green plants do.

➤ What will happen to celery stalks placed in water with food coloring, with dissolved salt, or with dissolved sugar? You can see what happens to the red coloring. How can you detect whether salt or sugar have moved up into the celery stalk?

➤ Does the temperature of water make a difference in the rate of speed at which red food coloring will travel in a white carnation?

➤ What happens to algae growth if you vary the concentration of salt in the water?

➤ How does acidity or alkalinity affect the time it takes for various seed coats (such as acorns) to break?

➤ Use bean seeds to determine which pH maximizes growth.

➤ Will bread mold grow on something other than bread?

➤ Does playing music or talking to plants make a difference in plant growth?

➤ Show how you can arrange to have your plant watered while you are away by making a wick with wire and strips of cloth. Push one end of the wick into the soil of a potted plant. Put the other end in a jar of water set next to the plant. Experiment with the amount of cloth that needs to be wrapped around the wire to transfer water.

➤ If you put several similar plants close together in their pots in a circle outdoors, will the center plants differ from the outside plants in their growth?

➤ Use a clear glass, wet sand or dirt, and seeds against the glass to demonstrate whether it makes any difference if seeds are planted right side up, upside down, or on their sides.

➤ Does temperature affect the germination time of bean seeds?

➤ Devise a chemical test to show whether or not vitamin C is present in a variety of foods.

➤ Devise an experiment showing dehydration and reconstitution of some fruits and/or vegetables.

Selected bibliography

Ardley, Neil. 1991. *The science book of things that grow*. San Diego, CA: Harcourt, Brace, Jovanovich.

Baily, Donna. 1990. *Forests*. Austin, TX: Steck-Vaughn Library.

Baker, Wendy and Andrew Haslam. 1993. *Plants: a creative hands-on approach to science*. New York, NY: Aladdin Books.

Bates, Jeffrey. 1991. *Seeds to plants*. New York, NY: Gloucester Press.

Other possible topics for investigation in botany

Becklake, John. 1991. *Food and farming*. New York, NY: Gloucester Press.

Bender, Lionel. 1988. *Plants*. New York, NY: Gloucester Press.

Bonnet, Robert L. 1991. *Botany: 49 more science fair projects*. Blue Ridge Summit, PA: TAB Books.

Bonnet, Robert L. 1990. *Environmental science: 49 science fair projects*. Blue Ridge Summit, PA: TAB Books.

Bourgeois, Paulette. 1990. *The amazing dirt book*. Reading, MA: Addison-Wesley.

Brooks, Felicity. 1991. *Protecting trees and forests*. Tulsa, OK: EDC Publishing.

Burnie, David. 1989. *Plant*. New York, NY: Knopf.

Byles, Monica. 1994. *Experiment with plants*. Minneapolis, MN: Lerner Publications.

Catherall, Ed. 1992. *Exploring plants*. Austin, TX: Raintree Steck-Vaughn Library.

Challand, Helen J. 1991. *Vanishing forests*. Chicago, IL: Children's Press.

Cochrane, Jennifer. 1987. *Plant ecology*. New York, NY: The Bookwright Press.

Coldrey, Jennifer. 1987. *Discovering flowering plants*. New York, NY: Bookwright Press.

Dowden, Anne Ophelia Todd. 1984. *From flower to fruit*. New York, NY: Crowell.

Facklam, Howard and Margery Facklam. 1990. *Plants: extinction or survival?* Hillside, NJ: Enslow.

Gibbons, Gail. 1991. *From seed to plant*. New York, NY: Holiday House.

Greenaway, Theresa. 1991. *Woodland trees*. Austin, TX: Steck-Vaughn.

Hare, Tony. 1990. *Rainforest destruction*. New York, NY: Gloucester Press.

Heller, Ruth. 1984. *Plants that never bloom*. New York, NY: Grosset & Dunlap.

Janulewicz, Mike. 1984. *Plants*. New York, NY: Gloucester Press.

Jordan, Helene J. 1992. *How a seed grows*. New York, NY: HarperCollins.

Kendra, Margaret. 1992. *Science Wizardry for kids*. New York, NY: Barrons.

Kerrod, Robin. 1990. *Plants in action*. New York, NY: Marshall Cavendish Corp.

Lambert, Mark. 1991. *Farming and the environment*. Austin, TX: Steck-Vaughn.

Lammert, John. 1992. *Plants*. Vero Beach, FL: Rourke.

Lawlor, Elizabeth P. 1993. *Discover nature close to home: things to know and things to do*. Harrisburg, PA: Stackpole Books.

Lerner, Carol. 1989. *Plant families*. New York, NY: Morrow Junior Books.

Markmann, Erika. 1991. *Grow it!: an indoor/outdoor gardening guide for kids*. New York, NY: Random House.

Morgan, Nina. 1993. *The plant cycle*. New York, NY: Thomson Learning

Overbeck, Cynthia. 1982. *Carnivorous plants*. Minneapolis, MN: Lerner Publications Co.

Overbeck, Cynthia. 1982. *How seeds travel*. Minneapolis, MN: Lerner Publications Co.

Pearce, Q. L. 1989. *Wondrous plant & earth experiments*. New York, NY: Tor.

Pringle, Laurence P. 1983. *Being a plant*. New York, NY: Crowell.

Raines, Kenneth G. 1989. *Nature projects for young scientists*. New York, NY: Franklin Watts.

Schoonmaker, Peter K. 1990. *The Living Forest*. Hillside, NJ: Enslow Publishers.

Stidworthy, John. 1991. *Flowers, trees & other plants*. New York, NY: Random House.

Suzuki, David T. 1991. *Looking at plants*. New York, NY: Wiley.

Taylor, Barbara. 1992. *Green thumbs up!: the science of growing plants*. New York, NY: Random House.

Walker, Lois. 1991. *Get growing!: exciting indoor plant projects for kids*. New York, NY: Wiley.

Wellnitz, William R. 1991. *Science in your backyard*. Blue Ridge Summit, PA: TAB Books.

Wellnitz, William R. 1990. *Science magic for kids: 68 simple and safe experiments*. Blue Ridge Summit, PA: TAB Books.

Wexler, Jerome. 1987. *Flowers, fruits, seeds*. New York, NY: Prentice Hall Books for Young Readers.

Wyler, Rose. 1986. *Science fun with peanuts and popcorn*. New York, NY; Julian Messner.

Wood, Robert M. 1991. *39 easy plant biology experiments*. Blue Ridge Summit, PA: TAB Books.

7

Possible projects in earth science and geography

The general area of earth science lends itself to a great many interesting science fair projects, including those that involve geography as well as the areas of geology, meteorology, conservation, global changes, and extinctions. The following are just a few possibilities for you to consider.

Everyone knows that the earth turns around the sun, and that one complete revolution makes a 24-hour day. But it might be interesting to plan a demonstration to show this by making a kind of earth rotation speedometer.

⚇ Experiment 12:
An earth rotation speedometer
Category: Earth science, grades 4–5

Materials needed: Chair, magnifying glass, sheet of white poster board, watch with second hand, a bright sunny day.

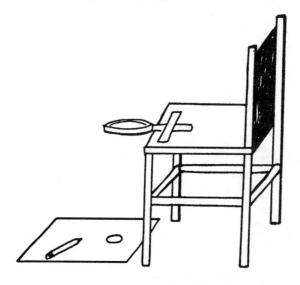

1. The purpose of your experiment is to show a way to measure the number of minutes in a day.
2. The hypothesis. A speedometer can be made using sunlight to indicate how long it takes the earth to travel half a degree of a circle.
3. The procedure. Take a chair outside in the bright sunlight. Tape the handle of a large magnifying glass to the seat of the chair so that the lens hangs over the edge of the chair. Put a sheet of white poster board on the ground, placed so that the magnifying glass casts a sharp light image on the paper. (You might have to raise the paper closer to the magnifying glass or raise the chair farther from the paper to achieve this sharp image.)
4. Data gathering. Draw a little circle around the spot of light that is on the paper. Write down the exact time that you are making this observation. Wait until the light entirely leaves the circle that you have drawn. Write down the exact time that the circle is empty of the bright light.
5. The results. Now you are ready for some mathematics. When the spot of light moves fully out of the circle on your paper, the earth has travelled ½ degree of its 360 degrees. There are 720 one-half degrees in 360 degrees. If you multiply the time it took for the light spot to move out of the circle by 720, you will find out how many minutes long a day really is.
6. The conclusion. Was your hypothesis correct? Can you use the sun to make an accurate earth rotation speedometer?

A favorite study in the general area of earth science is geology. Almost everyone is fascinated with rocks. Some people are attracted to gem stones and wonder where they are found and what makes them so valuable. Others like the rocks that they find in backyards or when out on hikes. These might have interesting colors or shapes.

Rocks are different in many ways. Some have been smoothed by tumbling about in rivers. Some are so soft that you can crumble them between your fingers. One way in which rocks differ is their hardness. You can carry out a simple science fair experiment to demonstrate this.

Experiment 13: The hardness of rocks
Category: Geology (earth science), grades 2–3

Materials needed: A metal nail file; an empty glass baby-food jar; some pennies; samples of rocks such as quartz, talc, calcite, hematite, pyrite, and gypsum.

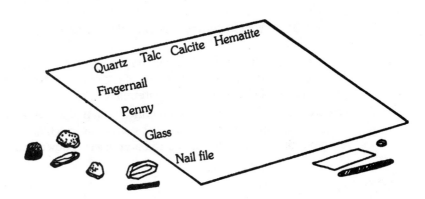

1. The purpose of your experiment is to demonstrate that rocks have different degrees of hardness.
2. The hypothesis. A scale of hardness of rocks can be made by using different types of rocks and showing whether or not they are hard enough to scratch different surfaces.
3. The procedure. Gather a group of mineral samples such as quartz, talc, calcite, hematite, pyrite, gypsum, etc. It would be fun to try to collect these yourself and to identify them. You might need to consult with some "rock hounds" in your area to assist in your identification. Or you might buy identified specimens at a rock shop.
   • Make a chart on a large sheet of poster board. List across the top of your chart each type of mineral that you are going to test. Down the left side of the chart, list the tests that you are going to use: fingernail, penny, glass, nail file.
4. Data gathering. For each specimen you will conduct four tests and will record "yes" or "no" as you find the answers to these questions: Can you scratch the rock with your fingernail? Can you scratch it with a penny? Will the rock specimen scratch the glass of a baby food jar? Will it scratch the nail file?
5. The results. Depending on the rock specimens that you use, you will find some that are too hard for you to scratch with your own fingernail, some that will scratch glass, etc. Using this information, you can arrange your rocks according to a scale of hardness.
6. The conclusion. Was your hypothesis correct? Can you use a "scratch test" to demonstrate the difference in hardness of rocks?

One of the major sets of skills to learn in geography is becoming proficient with maps. Because maps are flat, a way had to be found to indicate on maps the steepness of mountains. These maps are known as *topographic maps*. If you look at a topographic map, you will see a series of contour lines. A contour line connects all points at the same elevation. Where the lines are close together, the slope is steeper. This next exercise will help you prepare a science fair display showing the elevation of a mountainous area.

Experiment 14: Making a contour map
Category: Geography (earth science), grades 4–6

 Materials needed: Modeling clay, thin metal rod, deep bowl, ruler, toothpick, water.

1. The purpose of your experiment is to explain contour lines on topographic maps.
2. The hypothesis. If contour lines on a topographic map connect areas of the same elevation, an accurate topographic map can be constructed by using a model of a mountain and watermarks.
3. The procedure. To make your own contour map of a mountain, first mold a small mountain out of clay. Make it somewhat irregular in shape, like a real mountain. Take a thin metal rod and insert it down into the middle

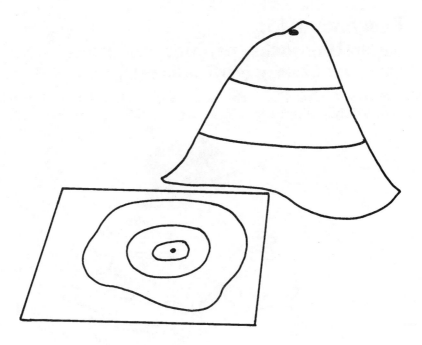

of the mountain, from top to bottom. Remove the rod. The hole left by the rod now marks the center of the mountain.

4. Data gathering. Set the clay mountain in a deep bowl. Stand a ruler in the bowl and pour in enough water so that the water measures 1 inch deep. Use a toothpick to draw the waterline on the surface of your clay mountain. Cut the waterline fairly deeply into the clay so that it is easy to see.

   • Then add another inch of water. Mark the waterline again. Continue doing this until you reach the top of the mountain.

   • Remove the mountain from the bowl. Use a piece of monofilament to slice off the top of the mountain along the line you cut with your toothpick. Trace this top piece of your model mountain carefully onto a sheet of paper. In addition to the outline, be sure to mark the center hole.

   • Now slice off another piece of the mountain at the next watermark, which you indicated with your toothpick line. Lining up the center holes, trace this shape on your sheet of paper. Continue the process until you have made an accurate map of your mountain.

5. The results. Once you place the layers of your mountain back together again, matching up the center holes, you will have both the mountain and an accurate topographic map of it to display. You could also make a "key" in which each inch might represent a raise of 500 feet. You would then know how many feet a mountain climber would need to climb to reach the top of your model mountain.

6. The conclusion. Was your hypothesis correct? Were you able to demonstrate the principle behind the contour lines on topographic maps?

Experiment 14: Making a contour map

Experiment 15:
Separating rocks, pebbles, and sand
Category: Geology (earth science), grades K–3

Materials needed: Piece of wood 12 inches wide and 4 feet long; block of wood 6 inches tall; watering can; a mixture of dirt, sand, pebbles, and rocks.

1. The purpose of your experiment will be to show that the flow of water in a stream sorts materials in it by their size and weight.

2. The hypothesis. A running stream of water will separate materials by size and weight, moving the smallest and lightest objects the greatest distance.

3. The procedure. In a coffee can, mix together sand, soil, pebbles and rocks. Place your plank of wood on a table that you have covered with plastic. Put a block under one end of the wood to create a slope to the plank. Put the lower end of the plank in an empty plastic tub.
   • Carefully dump one-half of a coffee can of your dirt, sand, pebble, and rock mixture in the middle of the high end of your plank. Slowly pour water from your watering can onto the mixture. Some of the mixture will slide off the plank onto the covered table, but much of it will move slowly down the plank.

4. Data gathering. After you have poured the water, observe what is left on the plank. Make a sketch in your science notebook showing where the dirt, sand, small pebbles, and larger rocks are on the plank.

5. The results. The dirt has quickly washed down into the tub. The largest rocks are highest on the plank. Small pebbles and sand are in between.

6. The conclusion. Was your hypothesis correct? Did the running water separate the materials by size and weight so that the smallest and lightest bits (dirt and sand) were moved the greatest distance?

Experiment 16: Demonstrating how sedimentary rock is sometimes formed
Category: Geology (earth science), grades K–5

Materials needed: A tall, wide-mouthed jar with a screw top; a third of a jar of water; a bowl containing a mixture of 6 tablespoons of dirt, 6 tablespoons of sand, and 6 tablespoons of fine pebbles.

1. The purpose of your experiment is to demonstrate how sedimentary rocks are formed.

2. The hypothesis. If you shake a tall jar that is one-third filled with water and a mixture of sand, dirt, and small pebbles, the larger, heavier objects will settle to the bottom, and the lighter objects will rest on top, just beneath the surface of the water.

3. The procedure. Take a tall jar and fill it one-third full of water. Mix together in a bowl 6 tablespoon each of dirt, sand, and small pebbles.

Experiment 16: Demonstrating how sedimentary rock is sometimes formed

Pour the mixture into the tall jar. Screw on the lid and shake the jar vigorously. Then set the jar upright on a table.

4. Data gathering. Observe what happens. Each time that you make an observation, note the time and what you see. Do not move the jar, and make your observations over several days.

5. The results. You will notice that the pebbles settle to the bottom of the jar right away. Then the sand will form a layer, and finally the soil will form a layer. In time, the water above the soil might be almost clear again.

6. The conclusion. Was your hypothesis correct? Did the heavy, larger objects sink to the bottom, leaving the lightest-weight material on top? This is how sedimentary rock is formed. Materials are deposited by water. In time, if tremendous pressure or heat or both are applied to the deposits, the layers become hardened into rock.

Rocks are made from a mixture of minerals. For example, the salt that we eat is a mineral named halite. Growing salt crystals is not hard to do.

Experiment 17: Making crystals
Category: Geology (earth science), grades 1–3

 Materials needed: Pan for boiling water, water, table salt, sugar, two glass jars, two pieces of thick string, two flat Popsicle sticks.

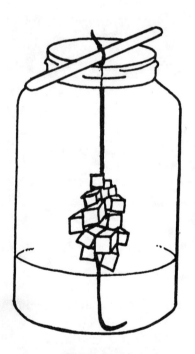

Salt crystals

Sugar crystals

1. The purpose of your experiment is to show that a salt crystal will have a different shape from a sugar crystal.

2. The hypothesis. As a solution of salt water and a solution of sugar water evaporate, the crystals that will form along a string suspended in each of the solutions can be identified by their shape.

3. The procedure. Bring a cup of water to a boil. Dissolve four tablespoons of salt in the water. Stir until all the salt is dissolved. Allow the pan of water to cool to room temperature. Then pour the water into a clean, tall, glass jar.

   • Tie a thick piece of string around the middle of a flat tongue depressor or Popsicle stick. Put the stick across the top of the jar. Dangle the string down through the salt water so that it touches the bottom of the jar. Put the jar in a warm place where it will not need to be moved.

   • Use a clean pan. Bring a cup of water to a boil. Dissolve four tablespoons of sugar in this water. Stir until all the sugar is dissolved. Allow the pan of sugar water to cool to room temperature. Then pour the water in a clean, tall, glass jar.

   • Repeat the procedure described previously for dropping a string down through the sugar water so that it touches the bottom of the jar. Then place the jar in a warm place where it will not need to be moved.

4. Data gathering. Each day, observe the jar of salt water and note what you see in your science log. Then observe the jar of sugar water and note what you see.

5. The results. After several days, you will see salt crystals forming along one string and sugar crystals forming along the other. If you examine these crystals under a magnifying glass, you will find that the salt crystals are perfect cubes and the sugar crystals are not cube-shaped.

6. The conclusion. Was your hypothesis correct? Did salt crystals have a shape different from the sugar crystals?

Experiment 18:
Relative humidity and evaporation
Category: Meteorology (earth science), grades 3–5

Materials needed: Two small strips of cloth, glass jar with lid, two pieces of string, two clothespins.

1. The purpose of your experiment is to show that relative humidity affects the rate of evaporation.

2. The hypothesis. A strip of cloth that is hung to dry in an open room inside a house will dry more quickly than a strip of cloth that dries inside a closed bottle with water sitting in the bottom of it.

3. The procedure. Fill a mason jar one-fourth full of water. Screw on the lid, and then let it sit for 30 minutes. Cut two strips of cloth that are approximately 1 inch by 3 inches in size. Soak both pieces of cloth in water, and then hang each up above the kitchen sink with a clothespin until they do not drip.

   • Drape one of the pieces of the wet pieces of cloth over the middle of a piece of string that is about 10 inches long. Open the jar. Carefully

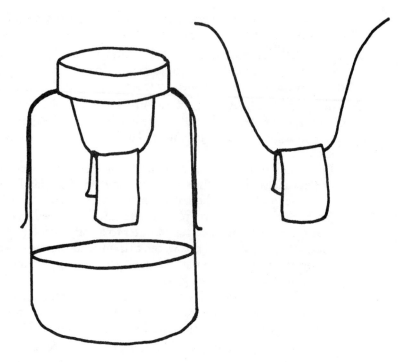

lower the string down into the jar so that the strip of cloth is hanging in the air above the water. Replace the lid.

• Use another piece of string to hang the other cloth strip somewhere in the house away from drafts.

4. Data gathering. Every fifteen minutes, check the piece of cloth that is drying on the string in the house. Note in your science log the times that you check on the cloth.

5. The results. When the piece of cloth hanging in the house feels quite dry, note the time. Then remove the second strip of cloth from the jar. Feel it. Is it dry?

6. The conclusion. Was your hypothesis correct? Did the amount of water vapor affect the drying time of the two pieces of cloth?

Experiment 19: Measuring relative humidity
Category: Meteorology (earth science), grades 4–5

 Materials needed: Two pieces of board, nails, two Fahrenheit thermometers, one strip of cotton cloth, one plastic glass filled with water, a piece of sturdy thread, one sturdy piece of cardboard about 2 feet square.

1. The purpose of your experiment is to demonstrate how to construct and read a simple hygrometer, which measures relative humidity in the air.

2. The hypothesis. If you fan the air around two thermometers, and if the bulb of one thermometer is wrapped in wet cloth that hangs like a wick in water, while another thermometer next to it has its dry bulb exposed to the air around it, the wet-bulbed thermometer will give a lower reading.

3. The procedure. Take two pieces of wood approximately 6 inches wide by 10 inches long. Use one piece of wood for the base. Nail the short edge of

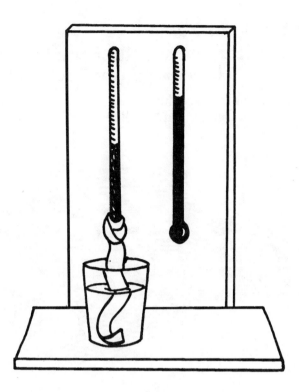

the second piece of wood to the base so that it stands upright in the middle of the board you are using as a base. Attach two Fahrenheit thermometers, side-by-side, on the upright pieces of wood.

- Dip a strip of cloth, approximately 1 inch wide by 10 inches long into water. Then wrap the strip of wet cloth around the bulb of one of the thermometers and tie it in place with a piece of thread. Let the rest of the strip of cloth dangle down into a plastic glass beneath it. Fill the plastic glass with water. (The strip of cloth will act like a wick.)

4. Data gathering. When everything is ready, take a sturdy sheet of cardboard and fan the air in front of the two thermometers. Check the temperature shown on each of the thermometers. Record each of the readings and note the time. Fan the thermometers again and take another set of readings. Repeat this three or four times.

5. The results. The lowest readings will be on the wet-bulb thermometer. If you repeated this experiment on days when weather conditions were quite different, what would your readings show?

6. The conclusion. Was your hypothesis correct? Did the thermometer with the wet cloth give a lower reading when you fanned the air around it than did the dry-bulbed thermometer?

It has often been said that everyone talks about the weather but no one does anything about it. And the local newspaper or television meteorologist who gives daily weather predictions usually comes in for considerable criticism or teasing for being pretty inaccurate. Have you ever wondered what percentage of weather predictions really are accurate? Here's a way to carry out an experiment to find out.

Experiment 19: Measuring relative humidity

Experiment 20:
How often are weather predictions accurate?
Category: Meteorology (earth science), grades 4–5

Materials needed: For this project you will need access to your local daily newspaper for October and May of the past year, and you will need graph and chart paper.

1. The purpose of your experiment is to answer the question, "What percentage of the time are local weather predictions accurate?"

2. The hypothesis. The weather predictions for high and low daily temperatures that were printed in the local paper last year were accurate more than 90% of the time during the months of October and May if accuracy is considered to be + or –3 degrees Fahrenheit.

3. The procedure. Through your local library or another source, locate the local newspaper weather predictions for high and low temperatures for each day of the months of October and May last year.

4. Data gathering. Using a different graph for each month, carefully record the high and low temperature predicted for each day in the paper and the actual recorded temperature.
   • You will have 62 sets of figures to work with (31 from each of the two months.) Consider the weather prediction to be accurate if both the actual high and low differ from the predicted high and low by 3 degrees or less.

5. The results. When you have finished checking your graphs, you will know how many times out of 62 the local weather prediction was accurate. From that, you can calculate the percentage of times the prediction was correct.

6. The conclusion. Was your hypothesis correct? Was the weather prediction accurate for 90% or more of the time?

Experiment 21: Soil conservation
Category: Conservation (earth science), grades 4–5

Materials needed: Two plastic tubs approximately 1 foot wide and 20 inches long, potting soil, grass seed, watering can, water, sheet of plastic, two plastic glasses, and an electric fan.

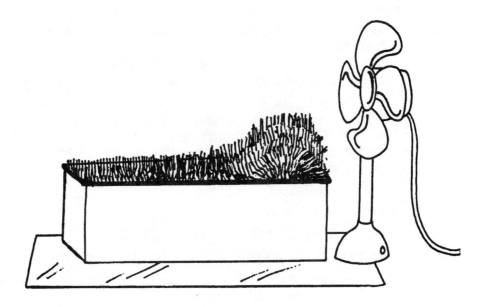

1. The purpose of your experiment is to demonstrate erosion by wind and water.
2. The hypothesis. Soil that does not have ground cover will be more easily eroded by both wind and water than soil that does have a ground cover growing in it.
3. The procedure. Fill each of your plastic containers half full of dirt. Then shape the dirt in each container with your hands so that there is a 6-inch-high plateau at one end of the container and then a slope going steeply down to the other end. Lightly sprinkle the dirt with water and pack it down in place. Set one container of dirt aside in a garage or other protected spot.
   - Plant grass seed thickly in the other container. Put it in a sunny spot and keep it well watered. Wait until you have a healthy crop of grass growing in the one container. Note in your science log when you planted the grass seed and how fast it grows.
4. Data gathering. When you have a good crop of grass growing in the one container, you are ready to do your experiment. First set the container with grass growing in it on a piece of plastic on a table. Plug in the fan. Let the fan blow across the container filled with grass for five minutes. Write down what you see. Collect any soil that was blown onto the sheet of plastic and put it in a plastic glass. Take the watering can. Pour water on the high-plateau end of the container. Use plenty of water so that it runs down the slope and collects at the bottom. Note what you see.

- Then take the container that you have been keeping in your garage and place the container on the plastic cloth. Let the fan blow across the container for five minutes. Write down what you see. Collect any soil that was blown onto the sheet of plastic and put it into a second plastic glass. Take the watering can. Pour water on the high-plateau end of the container. Use plenty of water so that it runs down the slope and collects at the bottom. Note what you see.

5. The results. Soil will be displaced by both the blowing air and the water. More soil will be displaced from the container that did not have a ground cover.

6. The conclusion. Was your hypothesis correct? Does a ground cover make a difference in the amount of soil erosion caused by both wind and water?

There is a lot of discussion through the news media about endangered species. Many schools provide courses of study in which endangered species are topics of discussion. Do you think that fifth graders are more aware of endangered species than the adults are in your community? By using a survey, you might be able to find out.

Experiment 22:
Awareness of endangered species
Category: Endangered species (earth science), grade 5

Materials needed: You will need to prepare 48 copies of a checklist and have access to 24 fifth graders and 24 adults.

Which species are endangered?

1. The purpose of your experiment is to discover whether fifth graders are more aware of endangered species than are the adults in their community.

2. The hypothesis. Because of the emphasis on studying endangered species in schools today, fifth graders will prove to be more accurate than adults when given a list of 10 creatures and asked to check just those that are on the endangered species list.

3. The procedure. Secure a list of endangered species from a recognized state or national wildlife organization. Choose four to six animals from that list. Choose enough other, fairly rare but not endangered animals to bring your list to a total of ten animals. You might list these at random or alphabetically. Put a box in front of each animal. Type the following directions above your list. "Please check all the boxes that appear in front of the names of animals currently on the endangered species list." Do not ask anyone to put their name on the sheet of paper. Run off 24 copies of your list on white paper and 24 copies on another color of paper.

4. Data gathering. With the permission of your teacher, give 25 fifth graders the white copies of your list. Allow a few minutes for the fifth graders to check the boxes of the animals that they think are endangered species. Using the lists that are on colored paper, get 24 adults to go through the same process. (You might ask relatives, friends, neighbors, or parents' coworkers to complete the list for you.)

5. The results. Carefully score each of the 48 sheets. The number right is the number of items that were correctly marked or left blank. Compare the fifth graders to the adults. Did one group do better than another?

6. The conclusion. Was your hypothesis correct? You predicted that the fifth graders would have a higher overall correct score than the adults. Did they?

Other possible topics for investigation in earth science and geography

➤ Are earthquakes correlated to sunspot activity?

➤ Make a model seismograph and show how this instrument works.

➤ How does heat affect air pressure? Design an experiment to demonstrate this.

➤ How does temperature affect the rate of sugar crystal growth?

➤ Display a rock collection that has been organized using a scale of hardness of rocks.

➤ Devise an experiment to show the force of freezing water.

➤ How could you measure the circumference of the earth?

➤ What affects erosion?

➤ Through a display, explain the rate of consumption of major fuels in the United States and how long reserves can be expected to last.

➤ Explain what a fossil is and display a fossil collection.

➤ Make a compass using a magnet, a steel needle, and thread.

➤ Use seeds enclosed in different liquids (distilled water, vinegar) to show the effect of acid rain.

➤ Some soils look light and others look dark. Can you determine pH by the lightness and darkness of soils?

➤ How does pH compare in topsoil and subsoil?

➤ Demonstrate how to find your latitude using the North Star.

➤ Devise a display to explain the difference between the magnetic axis of the earth and the true north and south axis.

➤ Devise an experiment using a large balloon to show how wind causes erosion and which materials are moved farthest by wind.

➤ How does slope affect soil erosion?

➤ How fast does water move through soil?

➤ Explain how underwater ridges are formed.

➤ Using plaster of paris, make an animal print and explain how real fossils are made.

➤ What affects the rate at which various sediments are deposited in water?

➤ Study and explain the difference of fluorescence between butter and oleomargarine by using a longwave ultraviolet light detector.

➤ What affects the acidity of rainwater?

➤ Compare the hardness of tap and rainwater.

➤ Make a simple barometer using a balloon, a straw, and a jar.

➤ Make and demonstrate a model of a geothermal steam engine.

➤ What affects the formation of frost?

➤ What affects evaporation?

➤ What substances can be added to the soil to make the soil more fertile?

➤ Do all minerals reflect light in the same way?

➤ Using white alum, grow crystals.

➤ Use a series of charts to show the five life zones and explain why different life exists in each zone.

➤ Various animals, particularly those of rain forests, are becoming extinct. Devise a display explaining how certain creatures are becoming extinct.

➤ How much water will various kinds of soil hold?

➤ Do earthworms prefer one type of soil to another?

➤ Can you devise an experiment using a thin layer of plaster of paris for "rock" to show how plants can break through rock?

Possible projects in earth science and geography

➤ Devise an experiment to show how magnetism can be used to identify certain minerals.

➤ The way in which a mineral breaks can help identify the mineral. Which minerals break with flat surfaces?

➤ Use charcoal and grape juice to show how you can clean dirty water.

Selected bibliography

Amsel, Sheri. 1993. *Rain forests*. Austin, TX: Raintree Steck-Vaughn.

Baker, Wendy. 1993. *Earth: a creative hands-on approach to science*. New York, NY: Aladdin Books.

Barnes-Svarney, Patricia L. 1991. *Born of heat and pressure: mountains and metamorphic rocks*. Hillside, NJ: Enslow Publishers.

Barrow, Lloyd H. 1991. *Adventures with rocks and minerals: geology experiments for young people*. Hillside, NJ: Enslow Publishing.

Bonnet, Robert L. and G. Daniel Keen. 1990. *Earth science: 49 science fair projects*. Blue Ridge Summit, PA: TAB Books.

Bourgeois, Paulette. 1990. *The amazing dirt book*. Reading, MA: Addison-Wesley.

Branley, Franklyn Mansfield. 1985. *Volcanoes*. New York, NY: Crowell.

Catherall, Ed. 1990. *Exploring soil and rocks*. Austin, TX: Steck-Vaughn.

Cleeve, Roger. 1990. *The earth*. Englewood Cliffs, NJ: J. Messner.

Cohen, Daniel. 1993. *Prehistoric animals*. New York, NY: Dell.

Cooper, Kay. 1990. *Where in the world are you? A guide to looking at the world*. New York, NY: Walker & Company.

Corbishley, Mike. 1990. *Detecting the past*. New York, NY: Gloucester Press.

Cox, Shirley. 1992. *Earth science*. Vero Beach, FL: Rourke.

Criswel, Susie Gwen. 1993. *Nature through science and art*. Blue Ridge Summit, PA: TAB Books.

Gay, Kathlyn. 1993. *Caretakers of the earth*. Hillside, NJ: Enslow Publishing.

Hare, Tony. 1990. *Greenhouse effect*. New York, NY: Gloucester Press.

Hilston, Paul. 1993. *A field guide to planet earth: projects for reading rocks, rivers, mountains, and the forces that shape them*. Chicago, IL: Chicago Review Press.

Jennings, Terry J. 1989. *The earth*. Freeport, NY: M. Cavendish.

Lye, Keith. 1991. *Rocks, minerals and fossils*. Englewood Cliffs, NJ: Silver Burdett Press.

Markle, Sandra. *Digging deeper: investigations into rocks, shocks, quakes, and other earthy matters*. New York, NY: Lothrop, Lee & Shepard Books.

Marner, Tom. 1990. *Rocks*. New York, NY: M. Cavendish.

Miller, Christina G. 1991. *Jungle rescue: saving the new world tropical rain forests*. New York, NY: Atheneum.

Mutel, Cornelia Fleischer. 1991. *Our endangered planet, tropical rain forests*. Minneapolis, MN: Lerner Pub..

Parker, Steve. 1993. *Rocks and minerals*. New York, NY: Dorling Kindersley.

Patent, Dorothy Hinshaw. 1993. *Habitats: Saving Wild Places*. Hillside, NJ: Enslow Publishers.

Other possible topics for investigation in earth science ◄

Patent, Dorothy Hinshaw. 1991. *The challenge of extinction*. Hillside, NJ: Enslow Publications.

Pearce, Q. L. 1993. *Strange science: planet earth*. New York, NY: Tom Doherty Associates.

Pearce, Q. L. 1989. *Wondrous plant and earth experiments*. New York, NY: Tor.

Rybolt, Thomas R. 1993. *Environmental experiments about land*. Hillside, NJ: Enslow Publishers.

Schlein, Miriam. 1991. *Let's go dinosaur tracking*. New York, NY: HarperCollins.

Seddon, Tony. 1987. *Physical world*. Garden City, NY: Doubleday.

Silverstein, Alvin. 1993. *Saving endangered animals*. Hillside, NJ: Enslow Publishers.

Smith, Bruce G. 1992. *Geology projects for young scientists*. New York, NY: Franklin Watts.

Snow, Theodore P. 1990. *Global change*. Chicago, IL: Children's Press.

Srogi, Lee Ann. 1989. *Start collecting rocks and minerals*. Philadelphia, PA: Running Press.

Taylor, Paul D. *Fossil*. 1990. New York, NY: Knopf.

Van Cleave, Janice Pratt. *Janice VanCleave's earth science for every kid*. New York, NY: J. Wiley.

Van Cleave, Janice Pratt. *200 gooey, slippery, slimy, weird, and fun experiments*. New York, NY: Wiley.

Wellnitz, William R. 1992. *Science in your backyard*. Blue Ridge Summit, PA: TAB Books.

Whyman, Kathryn. 1989. *Rocks and minerals*. New York, NY: Gloucester Press.

Wood, Robert W. 1992. *Science for kids: 39 easy geography activities*. Blue Ridge Summit, PA: TAB Books.

Wood, Robert W. 1991. *Science for kids: 30 easy geology experiments*. Blue Ridge Summit, PA: TAB Books.

Wood, Robert W. 1991. *Science for kids: 30 easy meteorology experiments*. Blue Ridge Summit, PA: TAB Books.

Yolen, Jane. 1993. *Welcome to the green house*. New York, NY: G. P. Putnam.

Zike, Dinah. 1993. *The earth science book: activities for kids*. New York, NY: John Wiley & Sons.

8

Possible projects in engineering

The broad field of engineering presents many possibilities for science fair projects. Some of these experiments will deal with building structures. Some will involve wind and water. Others will include the use of electricity. As in any of the science explorations mentioned in this book, safety is always a primary concern. Students should always work with appropriate adult supervision.

Students who are especially interested in some aspect of engineering might also want to review the chapter on physical science because these two areas somewhat overlap. This chapter is designed to help a young scientist focus on applying many of the principles of physics to some type of actual construction and design.

Learning about bridges can be a fascinating study. Bridges have been built for thousands of years. Some are very simple. Perhaps you have gone hiking in the woods and have walked across a big log that someone put across a stream to form a bridge for hikers. Other bridges are very complex. After doing some reading about bridge construction, you might decide on a science fair project that will bring your skills and understanding of the principles of engineering into play.

 ## Experiment 23:
Comparing the strength of beam and arch bridges
Category: Engineering, grades 3–5

Materials needed: Poster board, two thick books, a clear plastic tub or small box, several marbles of the same size and weight.

1. The purpose of your experiment is to answer the question, "Which will hold more weight, a simple beam bridge or an arched bridge?"
2. The hypothesis. A bridge that is constructed with an arch put beneath a simple beam bridge to cross a span will strengthen the bridge so that it will hold more weight.

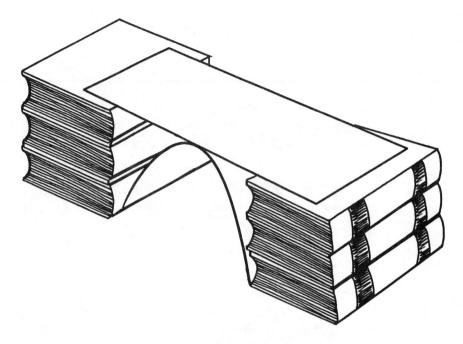

3. The procedure. Cut a piece of poster board that is 6 inches wide and 1 foot long. Using two books of equal thickness (such as volumes of an encyclopedia), put them flat on a table, side by side. Move them apart so that there is about 9 inches of distance between them. Place your piece of poster board so that it spans the distance between the two books with approximately 1½ inches of the poster board resting on the surface of the book on each side.

4. Data collection. Using a clear plastic tub or box placed in the middle of your bridge, add marbles until the cardboard beam bridge bends and touches the table. Count the number of marbles in the tub.

   • Now take another piece of poster board and cut it so that it is 6 inches wide and 11 inches long. Place this strip between the two books that are 9 inches apart, bending the strip of poster board upward into an arch and wedging the bottom of each side between the two heavy books. (You might need to do a little trimming and adjusting so that this arch fits snugly. Now place the first piece of poster board across the books again, resting on top of your arched bridge.

   • Using a clear plastic tub or small box, add the same number of marbles that you used before, and place the tub or box in the center of the bridge. Then, one by one, add additional marbles. How many more marbles can you add before the bridge collapses?

5. The results. By putting an arch beneath the simple span bridge, you have strengthened it. The weight of your marbles pushed the arch in on itself. This compressed the paper.

6. The conclusion. Was your hypothesis correct? Did placing an arch beneath the span strengthen it so that it would support more weight than before?

Experiment 24:
Does the position of a beam affect its strength?
Category: Engineering, grades 4–5

Materials needed: A plastic drop cloth, two small tables of the same height, a short length of rope, a bucket, sand, four C-clamps, four small blocks of wood that are 2 inches on a side, two pieces of wood that are ¼ inch thick by 2 inches wide and 2 feet long, scales.

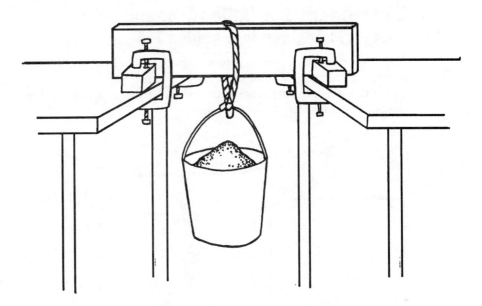

1. The purpose of your experiment is to explore the relationship between the way a piece of wood for a bridge is positioned and its strength.
2. The hypothesis. If identical boards span the distance between two tables, the board that is placed on its narrow edge will prove stronger than the board that is placed flat across the span.
3. The procedure. Put down a drop cloth. Place two small tables on the cloth so that they are above twenty inches apart. Use a C-clamp and blocks of wood to secure your long strip of wood between the two tables. Be sure that the wood can't move. Use the short length of rope to secure an empty bucket in the center of your bridge. Add sand to the bucket until the bridge bends downward and breaks.
4. Data gathering. Weigh the bucket and sand and record this amount. Then repeat the process above using the second piece of wood. This time, put the piece of wood on its edge. Use 4 C-clamps and blocks, one on the right and left of each end of the strip of wood to keep it from moving.
   • Again use the short length of rope to secure an empty bucket in the center of your bridge. Add sand to the bucket until the bridge bends downward and breaks. Weigh the bucket and sand and record this amount.

Experiment 24: Does the position of a beam affect its strength

5. The results. Although the boards were exactly the same dimensions, one could hold more weight than another when placed across a span because of the way in which each board was positioned.

6. The conclusion. Was your hypothesis correct? Did placing the board with its narrowest edge facing down toward the floor allow it to hold more weight before breaking than placing it with the flat side down?

You have learned something about wooden beams and their strength. Inflated balloons can provide you with the material for another interesting structural experiment.

 # Experiment 25: Balloon beams
Category: Engineering, grades 3–5

Materials needed: A long balloon; tape; two boxes of equal size; a piece of string; a paper clip; several objects of different weights such as nuts, bolts, spools of thread, fishing sinkers, etc., each tied with a loop of thread so that they can be hung from the paper clip.

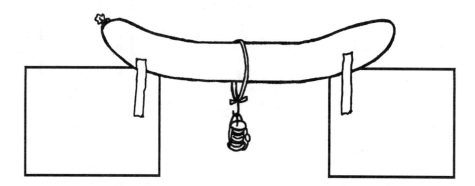

1. The purpose of your experiment is to answer the question, "Can something as light as a balloon be used to support weight?"

2. The hypothesis. If a balloon is filled with air and placed as a bridge span between two boxes, it will support several times its own weight before collapsing.

3. The procedure. Blow up a long, slender balloon. Tie it securely so that no air will escape. Attach the balloon with tape securely to two cardboard boxes so that the balloon spans the space between the two boxes like a bridge.
   • Tie a string loosely around the middle of the balloon. Allow the ends of the string to dangle down about 2 inches. Slip a paper clip on to the ends of the string and tie a knot. Open the paper clip so that it forms a sort of hook.
   • The paper-clip "hook" is now dangling down in the air in the middle of the span. Try attaching a variety of weights, such as spools of thread or fishing sinkers from the paper clip. How much weight will the balloon bridge support?

4. Data gathering. Record the amount of weight that you can suspend from the paper clip before the balloon bridge eventually collapses.

5. The results. The balloon becomes stiff because the internal air pressure acts in all directions on the balloon's walls so that it is tensed both lengthwise and crosswise. This allows it to become a bridge, strong enough to support considerable weight.

6. The conclusion. Was your hypothesis correct? By blowing up a balloon, can you create a bridge that will support several times its own weight?

Just as arches are used in bridges, domes are often used in buildings. This next experiment will help you understand how a dome works. Whatever it is made of, a dome is a series of arches set around a vertical axis. An egg is a kind of dome that is quite strong for its size and weight.

Experiment 26: Domes and cubes
Category: Engineering, grades 2–5

Materials needed: A board 6 inches wide and 1 foot long, two eggs, four egg cups, cotton batting, two square cardboard boxes.

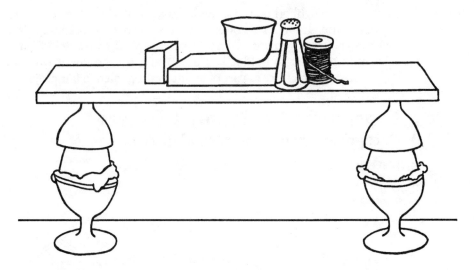

1. The purpose of your experiment is to determine whether or not a dome is stronger than a cube.

2. The hypothesis. If domes and cubes of approximately the same weight are used to support a board, the domes will support more weight than the cubes.

3. The procedure. Weigh an uncooked egg and two egg cups. Find two identical cardboard boxes that each weigh the same amount as an egg and two egg cups. Set the two cardboard boxes about 10 inches apart. Support your 1-foot-long board across them.
   • Use cotton to pad the inside of your four egg cups. Put each end of both uncooked eggs into a padded egg cup.

4. Data gathering. Add weight to the board that is resting on the cardboard boxes. Continue to add weight until the boxes collapse. Weigh and record the amount of weight that the two boxes supported.
   • Now balance the board on top of the pair of uncooked eggs cradled between the padded egg cups set 10 inches apart. Add weight to the

board that is resting on the eggs. Continue to add weight until they break. Weigh and record the amount of weight that the uncooked eggs supported.

5. The results. Eggs will support more weight than cubes. (Depending on how heavy you are, you might be able to stand on the board resting on the uncooked eggs without breaking them!)

6. The conclusion. Was your hypothesis correct? Does a dome bear more weight than a cube?

Engineers not only have to be concerned about the force of the load and of the structure's weight pushing down, but they sometimes need to consider the force of the wind. High-rise buildings have posed special problems for engineers. Very tall buildings are pushed with a strong force when winds blow.

In designing very tall buildings, engineers have used what they know about strong bridge construction and the way sturdy triangles are used as supports. Use of this type of design, for example, can be seen in the structure of the Sears Building in Chicago.

In your own neighborhood, you might have noticed workers putting a roof on top of a house. Triangles are often used to support roofs because this makes for a very stable arrangement. When force is applied to triangle figures, all the sides work together to hold it in place. You can experiment with stability of shapes used in structures as part of an interesting science fair project.

Experiment 27: Sturdy triangles
Category: Engineering, grades 2–5

Materials needed: Straight pins, drinking straws.

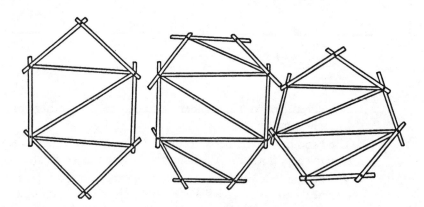

1. The purpose of your experiment is to answer the question, "How can a structure be made stable?"

2. The hypothesis. Two-dimensional squares, pentagons, and hexagons made of straws can be made stable using the fewest additional straws by adding straws that will form triangles within the shapes.

3. The procedure. Pin four straws together to form a square. Pull or push on the sides, and you will see that the square is not rigid. It is easily bent out

of shape. Experiment using just one more straw placed in such a way that the square does not move to and fro. Save the figure that is most stable.

- Pin five straws together to form a pentagon. What is the fewest number of straws you can add to make the figure stable? Set this figure aside.
- Now pin six straws together to form a hexagon. What is the fewest number of straws you can add to make this figure stable? Set this figure beside the others. Repeat this same procedure with a heptagon and an octagon.

4. Data gathering. Look at each of the five figures that you constructed. Compare all of them. Is there a pattern about how many straws are needed to keep each two-dimensional figure from moving to and fro?

5. The results. Each of the figures has been divided into a series of triangles. If you count the number of sides of the figure and the number of triangles in the figure, you will find that there is a pattern. The number of triangles will be two less than the number of sides.

6. The conclusion. Was your hypothesis correct? In two-dimensional figures, are triangles the best way to make them stable?

Engineers are involved in many areas other than buildings and bridges. They frequently design machines to efficiently do work. Hydraulic machines such as pumps and braking systems contain a liquid under pressure. The liquid pushes on a piston, producing enough power to operate the machine.

Experiment 28: Liquid pressure power
Category: Engineering, grades 2–5

Materials needed: Several books, a piece of clear plastic tubing about 3 feet long, a strong plastic bag, a funnel, a 2-quart pitcher, and tap water.

1. The purpose of your experiment is to answer the question, "Can water pressure be used to lift weight?"
2. The hypothesis. If water is poured down a tube into an empty plastic bag placed beneath three heavy books on a table, the pressure of the water will force the books to rise off the table.
3. The procedure. Place a strong plastic bag on a table and place three books on top of the bag. Use a rubber band to fasten a piece of plastic tubing securely into the neck of the bag. At the other end of the tubing, attach the tube to the narrow end of a funnel. Hold the funnel and tubing about 2 feet above the books. Take a pitcher of water and slowly but steadily pour water into the funnel so that it runs down the tube to the plastic bag.
4. Data gathering. Watch what happens when you pour the water into the funnel. Does it make a difference how high or how low you hold the funnel? Experiment with different heights.
5. The results. Record what you see when you pour water into a funnel that is held about 6 inches above the books. Then record what happens when you pour water into a funnel that is held about 1 foot above the books. Repeat, holding the funnel about 2 feet above the books.
6. The conclusion. Was your hypothesis correct? Was the water under pressure able to lift the heavy weight of the books?

Henri Coanda made an interesting discovery when he built and flew a flying machine in 1910. It is called the Coanda Effect. You can make a simple science fair project to demonstrate this effect.

Experiment 29: The Coanda Effect
Category: Engineering, grades 3–5

Materials needed: A candle in a sturdy candle holder, a match, a soda straw, and a large can or jar.

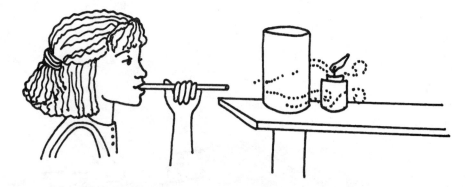

1. The purpose of your experiment is to answer the question, "Does air follow the wall contour when it is released next to the surface of the wall?"
2. The hypothesis. Air blown through a straw at the front of a jar will follow the contour of the jar and blow out a candle that is placed squarely behind the jar.
3. The procedure. Place a lighted candle in a sturdy candle holder on a table directly behind a large jar or can. Bend down so that your face is level with

the table. Hold the straw at the front side of the can or jar and blow into it. The air stream will curve around the can or jar to blow out the candle.

4. Data gathering. Observe what happens when you blow into the straw.

5. The results. The increased velocity of air near the jar causes a decrease of pressure. The pressure of the still air keeps the moving air near the glass until the velocity decreases. This allows the air to curve around the jar and blow out the candle.

6. The conclusion. Was your hypothesis correct? Did air flow around the curve of the jar? Did you demonstrate the Coanda Effect?

You can also notice this effect when you pour water from a glass or pour tea from a teapot. The water or tea tends to run down the side. In this case, the liquid is also attracted by surface tension.

Here's another idea for a project to show wind force. It demonstrates what might happen to windows in a high rise building that is hit by heavy winds.

Experiment 30: Wind pressure and vacuum
Category: Engineering, grades 3–5

  Materials needed: An electrical fan, a sturdy cereal or other cardboard box, a weight, a needle, and thread.

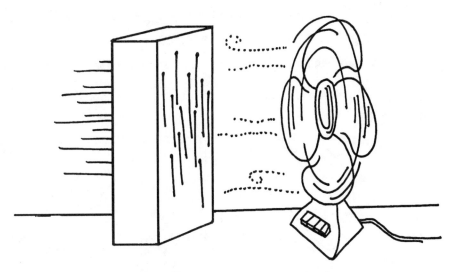

1. The purpose of your experiment is to answer the question, "What happens when wind blows against a structure?"

2. The hypothesis. When wind blows against a structure, there will be pressure on one side and a vacuum will be created on the other side.

3. The procedure. Using a large needle, thread about a dozen threads through a cereal or other cardboard box. Cut the threads to such a length so that the thread dangles down about 4 inches on both sides of the cereal box. Put a heavy weight inside the cereal box so that it will not blow over when a fan blows air against it.
   • Place the weighted cereal box on a table. Put the fan about 3 feet from the box and turn it on.

4. Data gathering. Observe and note what happens. You might want to make a sketch of what you see.

5. The results. The threads on the side of the cereal box closest to the fan will press down flat against the box due to the pressure of the moving air. On the far side of the box, however, the strings will stand out straight because of the vacuum that has been created by the air moving around the box.

6. The conclusion. Was your hypothesis correct? Did you show that a vacuum was created behind the structure when wind hit the structure from the other side?

If you live somewhere where it snows, you might have noticed how "quiet" the world seems on the morning after a snowstorm. This is because snow is in crystals that have millions of spaces. These spaces absorb sound.

But much of the time, machines and other factors cause our world to be very noisy. Engineers try to plan ways to reduce this irritating noise. They know that flat, hard surfaces reflect sound, while soft, porous surfaces absorb sound. Fabric is a good absorber. An empty auditorium, for example, will reflect far more sound than an auditorium filled with people wearing a variety of clothing. A room with drapes and carpeting will be quieter than a room with bare windows and tile floors. You can do a simple experiment to study soundproofing.

Experiment 31: Noisy rooms and quiet rooms
Category: Engineering, grades 4–5

Materials needed: A meter to measure sound; two wooden blocks; two rooms in a school that are about the same size and shape and that have the same kind of ceilings (one room should be carpeted, and one should not).

1. The purpose of your experiment is to answer the question, "Can noise in a room be reduced by the materials covering the floor, ceiling, and walls?"

2. The hypothesis. Sound, as measured by a sound meter, will be greatest in an empty room with no carpeting and least in a carpeted room with fabric wall hangings if the rooms are approximately the same size and have the same kind of ceilings.

3. The procedure. Using a sound meter, you will measure the sound produced when a friend bangs together two blocks of wood in different rooms while standing 8 feet from you.

4. Data gathering. You will need permission from your school administrator and custodian to carry out this experiment. First you will want to measure the sound in an uncarpeted, empty classroom. (Perhaps this could be done at a time when the room is emptied for cleaning.)

   • First, photograph the room from the doorway, showing as much of the interior as possible, including part of the floor. Ask a friend to sit near the middle of the room about 8 feet from you and bang together two blocks of wood while you watch the needle of the sound meter that you hold. Record the reading.

   • Then move into a classroom that has students, furniture, and carpeting in it. Photograph this room, as explained previously, while standing in the doorway. Have your friend sit 8 feet from you and bang together two blocks of wood while you watch the needle on the sound meter that you hold. Record the reading.

   • During a recess or noon hour, use masking tape to put blankets as best you can all around the walls of the classroom. After students have returned to the room, photograph the room again from the doorway. Be sure to show a wall that you have covered with blankets.

   • Have your friend sit 8 feet from you again and bang together the two blocks of wood while you watch the sound meter that you hold. Record the measurement.

5. The results. When you graph results from your three attempts at measuring sound, you should find differences in the amount of sound that has been absorbed or reflected.

6. The conclusion. Was your hypothesis correct? Did the empty room with no carpeting reflect sound the most and the blanketed room absorb the most sound?

Loud sounds are not always bad. Cars and homes are often fitted with a variety of devices to give off a loud warning alarm when someone enters without permission. The following information will help you to design your own simple burglar alarm.

Experiment 32:
Using an electrical circuit
to operate a burglar alarm
Category: Engineering, grades 4–5

Materials needed: An old briefcase or plastic case with handle, two pieces of scrap lumber, a 6-volt dry-cell battery, a bell, six nails, a coat hanger.

1. The purpose of your experiment is to design an electrical circuit that will set off a burglar alarm.

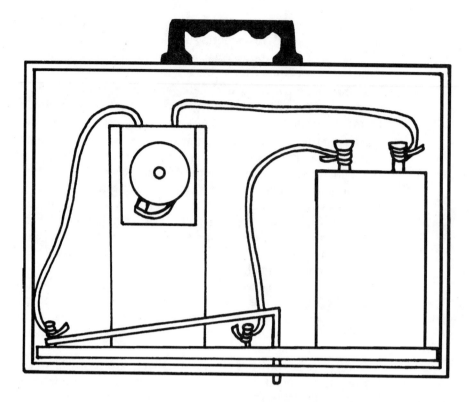

2. The hypothesis. A model of a simple burglar alarm can be fashioned out of materials using an electrical circuit to activate a bell.

3. The procedure. Cut a piece of scrap lumber to fit tightly in the bottom of a case. For our purposes, we will say that the bottom is 3 inches wide and 12 inches long. (You will need to adjust your measurements to fit the briefcase you are using.) Drill a ¼-inch hole through both the bottom of the case and this narrow board, centered and 7 inches from one end.

   - Hammer two broad-headed nails into this narrow piece of wood. One nail should be centered a ½ inch from the end farthest from the drilled hole. The second nail should be centered and 6 inches from the first nail and ½ inch from the hole you have drilled.
   - Attach a second piece of scrap lumber to a side of the bottom piece by using four nails. This second piece should be 6 inches wide and, when attached, should stand up about 8 inches high.
   - Mount a bell on the upright piece of wood. Run a wire from the bell to the broad-headed nail that is ½ inch from the end of the bottom piece of wood. Attach it. Run another wire from the bell to a 6-volt battery that rests on the bottom piece of wood at the end where there is no nail.
   - Run another wire from the 6-volt battery down to the nail on the bottom board that is just in front of the drilled hole. Fasten it in place beneath the nail head.
   - Make a switch from a piece of springy wire clothes hanger by bending it with a pliers to form the letter "L." Scrape off any coating on the clothes wire so that the ends are bare. Fasten the long end of the clothes hanger wire beneath the nail at the end of the wood, making contact with the wire that runs to the bell.

- Let the short end of the "L" stick down through the hole that you have drilled in the wood. Be sure that the short end of the coat hanger is long enough so that when the case rests on a low table-top, it sticks up slightly inside the bag so that the coat hanger does not make contact with the wire beneath it.
- Stick a piece of monopoly money into the briefcase so that it shows through when the briefcase is snapped shut. Add a sign to your briefcase that says, "One million dollars of funny money inside. Try to carry it away without setting off the alarm!"
- When someone picks up the case from the low table, the short end of the "L" clothes hanger wire will drop down through the hole and make contact with the wire that is fastened to the nail head. This will set off the bell. When the case is set back on the table, the short end of the "L" will be forced up again, losing contact with the wire, breaking the circuit, and so silencing the bell.

4. Data gathering. You will need to do some experimenting with the clothes hanger and with the bag you use to find the exact measurements that will allow the contact to be made and broken by having the "L" shaped coat hanger drop into the hole you have drilled.

5. The result. When wiring and switch adjustments are correct, a bell will go off when the soft briefcase is picked up and will stop when the soft briefcase is rested on the table top again.

6. The conclusion. Was your hypothesis correct? Did you demonstrate that a closed electrical circuit could be used to set off a simple burglar alarm?

Other possible topics for investigation in engineering

➤ Newton's third law states that every action has an equal but opposite reaction. Use a toy electric engine and a section of train track on rollers (such as round pencils) to demonstrate this.

➤ To demonstrate Newton's law that every action has an equal and opposite reaction, experiment with punching holes in a milk carton filled with water and held up by a string to form a spinning wheel.

➤ Build a machine that will separate large marbles from small ones.

➤ Use weights, clamps, two chairs, and yardsticks to demonstrate beam structure.

➤ Design and build a model of your ideal house.

➤ Build several balsa wood towers using different designs. Set a lightweight board on top of your tower. Use weights to see which design yields the strongest weight-bearing tower.

➤ Try building towers with cardboard or rolled newspapers or drinking straws or pipe cleaners. Use a plastic glass of water to test the designs of your different towers.

➤ Use a bag of rocks and a homemade wheelbarrow constructed from a shoe box, sticks, and an empty wooden spool to demonstrate how using a lever lets you move things with less effort.

➤ Design and build a beam bridge that will span 2 feet and that will support the weight of a brick. Try several designs. Which one works? Why?

➤ Make a homemade fan run by a handle that you can wind up to demonstrate the use of gears.

➤ Design your own hydraulic machine to show how you can raise a heavy weight with water.

➤ Devise a simple machine that will change circular motion into an up-and-down movement.

➤ Use strips of cardboard and paper fasteners to build a cantilever bridge. Try different designs. If you attached each end of the bridge to a box, what is the greatest distance you can span?

➤ Find out about and build a model of a Takenaka space truss and show how such a space truss can be used to support the roofs of sports arenas.

➤ Make a model suspension bridge using carpet thread and cardboard.

➤ Make a small concrete beam. Try making a reinforced beam. Devise an experiment to test the strength of your beams.

➤ Make a burglar alarm using a silk thread, a mouse trap, a battery, insulated doorbell wire, and a doorbell.

➤ Experiment with the shapes of paper airplanes. What shapes work best and why?

➤ Build a simple electromagnet.

➤ Make a model to demonstrate how a flywheel works.

➤ Show how you can make a paper bridge by pleating and folding the paper.

➤ Devise a way to convert wind energy into electricity.

➤ Make a model solar hot-water heater.

➤ Make a simple model of Edison's electric light by using a wide-mouthed jar with cover, battery, switch, a very thin strand of copper wire for a filament, nails, and hook-up wire.

➤ Using a flashlight battery, strips of copper, an iron nail, and a salt and vinegar solution, experiment with electroplating.

➤ Make an electroscope to indicate the presence of an electrical charge.

➤ Show how a front and back doorbell circuit works by connecting pushbutton switches in parallel with one another.

➤ What affects how well toothpaste removes denture stains?

➤ Do flaps increase an airplane's lifting power?

➤ What affects the load-bearing ability of a suspension bridge?

➤ Devise a series of experiments using a tin can with punched holes in a row at various intervals to investigate water pressure.

➤ The human skeleton is a structure. Make a model arm that will move by using cardboard and rubber bands.

➤ Design and make a lighthouse or an oil rig.

➤ Make a small windmill that will do work.

➤ How does wing shape affect an airplane's flight?

➤ Compare the strength of tunnels that have arched roofs with tunnels that have square roofs by building tunnels in sand using cardboard tubes and boxes.

➤ Make a crane with dowels, wood, and cardboard. Can you devise a pulley arrangement so that your crane can pick up a load?

➤ Use nails and a solution of copper sulfate to show how you can coat nails with metallic copper.

Selected bibliography

Ardley, Neil. 1984. *Force and strength*. New York, NY: Franklin Watts.

Ardley, Neil. 1992. *The science book of machines*. San Diego, CA: Harcourt, Brace, Jovanovich.

Arnold, Caroline. 1986. *The Golden Gate Bridge*. New York, NY: Franklin Watts.

Baker, Wendy. 1993. *Electricity: a creative hands-on approach to science*. New York, NY: Aladdin Books.

Berger, Melvin. 1989. *Switch on, switch off*. New York, NY: Crowell.

Boring, Mel. 1984. *Incredible constructions and the people who built them*. New York, NY: Walker.

Boyer, Edward. 1986. *River and canal*. New York, NY: Holiday House.

Boyston, Angela. 1991. *Buildings, bridges, and tunnels*. New York, NY: Warwick Press.

Carter, Polly. 1992. *The bridge book*. New York, NY: Simon & Schuster Books for Young Readers.

Cash, Terry. 1990. *175 more science experiments to amuse and amaze your friends: experiments! tricks! things to make!* New York, NY: Random House, 1990.

Catherall, Ed. 1990. *Exploring electricity*. Austin, TX: Steck-Vaughn Library.

Challand, Helen J. 1988. *Experiments with chemistry*. Chicago, IL: Children's Press.

Challenger, Jack. 1992. *My first batteries and magnets book*. New York, NY; Dorling Kindersley.

Churchill, E. Richard. 1990. *Building with paper*. New York, NY: Sterling Pub. Co.

Darling, David J. 1991. *Spiderwebs to sky-scrapers: the science of structures*. New York, NY: Dillon Press.

Denvonshire, Hilary. 1992. *Flight*. New York, NY: Franklin Watts.

Dixon, Malcolm. 1991. *Flight*. New York, NY: Bookwright Press.

Other possible topics for investigation in engineering ◀

Dixon, Malcolm. 1991. *Structures*. New York, NY: Bookwright Press.

Dunn, Andrew. 1993. *Bridges*. New York, NY: Thomson Learning.

Fitzpatrick, Julie. 1988. *Towers and bridges*. Englewood Cliffs, NJ: Silver Burdett Press.

Gaff, Jackie. 1991. *Buildings, bridges & tunnels*. New York, NY: Random House.

Gallimard, Jeunesse (trans.). 1992. *Airplanes and flying machines*. New York, NY: Scholastic.

Gardner, Robert. 1993. *Favorite Science Experiments*. New York, NY: Franklin Watts.

Goodwin, Peter. 1987. *Engineering projects for young scientists*. New York, NY: Franklin Watts.

Green, Charles. 1984. *All about crystal sets: how-to-build simple crystal set radios*. Freemont, CA: Allabout Books.

Harris, Jack C. 1988. *Dream cars*. Mankato, MN: Crestwood House.

Isaacson, Philip M. 1988. *Round buildings, square buildings, & buildings that wiggle like a fish*. New York, NY: Knopf.

Jennings, Terry J. 1993. *Planes, gliders, helicopters, and other flying machines*. New York, NY: Kingfisher Books, 1993.

Katz, Phyllis. 1992. *Great science fair projects*. New York, NY: Franklin Watts.

Kerrod, Robin. 1987. *Moving things*. Morristown, NJ: Silver Burdett Press.

Lewis, Alun. 1980. *Super structures*. New York, NY: Viking.

MacGregor, Anne. 1980. *Bridges: a project book*. New York, NY: Lothrop, Lee & Shepard Books.

Markle, Sandra. 1989. *Power up: experiments, puzzles, and games exploring electricity*. New York, NY: Atheneum.

Marshall, Ray and John Bradley. 1985. *The plane: watch it work by operating the moving diagrams!* New York, NY; Viking Kestral.

Millspaugh, Ben P. 1991. *Aviation and space science projects*. Blue Ridge Summit, PA: TAB Books.

Morgan, Sally. 1993. *Structures*. New York, NY: Facts on File.

Prochnow, Dave and Kathy. 1993. *Why? experiments for the young scientist*. Blue Ridge Summit, PA: TAB Books.

Rickard, Graham. 1987. *Bridges*. New York, NY: Bookwright Press.

Richards, Roy. 1990. *101 science tricks: fun experiments with everyday materials*. New York, NY: Sterling Pub. Co.

Robbins, Ken. 1991. *Bridges*. New York, NY: Dial Books.

Robson, Pam. 1992. *Air, wind, & flight*. New York, NY: Gloucester Press.

Salvadori, Mario George. 1990. *Art of construction: projects and principles for beginning engineers and architects*. Chicago, IL: Chicago Review Press.

Stein, R. Conrad. 1982. *The story of the Panama canal*. Chicago, IL: Childrens Press.

Taylor, Barbara. 1991. *Structures and materials*. New York, NY: Franklin Watts.

Walker, Ormiston H. 1989. *Experimenting with air and flight*. New York, NY: Franklin Watts.

Whyman, Kathryn. 1987. *Structures and materials*. New York, NY: Gloucester Press.

Williams, Brian. 1991. *Explore the world of marvelous machines*. Racine, WI: Western Publishing.

Williams, John. 1992. *Projects with electricity*. Milwaukee, WI: Gareth Stevens Children's Books.

Wood, Robert W. 1992. *Science for kids: 39 easy engineering experiments*. Blue Ridge Summit, PA: TAB Books.

Zubrowski, Bernie. 1991. *Blinkers and buzzers: building and experimenting with electricity and magnetism*. New York, NY: Morrow.

9
Possible projects in health and behavioral science

Studying about the human body, learning ways of maintaining good health and minimizing health hazards, and examining ways in which humans learn and behave are all topics that lend themselves well to a variety of science fair projects. Students could also investigate such topics as the senses, involuntary bodily actions, special organs, and environmental health hazards.

Air quality is a topic that is frequently in the news. *Particulate matter* refers to tiny particles in the air. When a volcano erupts, large quantities of particulate matter are released into the air. Sandstorms are another example of naturally released particles. But many human activities also result in the formation of particulate matter. Such things as automobile exhaust emissions or smoke from wood-burning stoves are ways that these particles are released into the air.

Many air particles are unhealthy and, in sufficient quantity, might even change the temperature of the earth by blocking out sunlight. This next experiment will show you how to measure the amount of light blocked by particulate matter in the air.

Experiment 33:
Measuring light blocked by particulates
Category: Health and behavioral science, grades 4–5

Materials needed: A slide projector, a photo light meter, two cups of flour, a flour sifter, a bowl.

1. The purpose of your experiment is to find out whether light is blocked by particulate matter in the air.
2. The hypothesis. If you measure the amount of light in an area and then stir up flour as particulate matter in the air in that area, the amount of light will be measurably reduced.
3. The procedure. Put a slide projector on a table. About 4 feet away, set a photo light meter. Point the light meter right at the light coming from the slide projector. Take readings of the light and record the data.

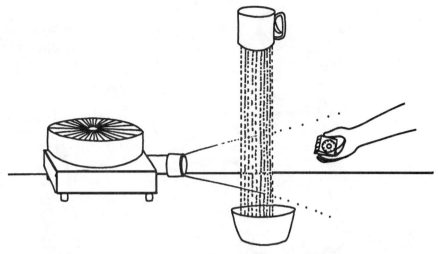

- Then take two cups of flour and put them in a flour sifter. Slowly sift the flour through the sifter into a bowl placed on the table between the slide projector and the photo light meter. The flour particles will make a sort of cloud.

4. Data gathering. Immediately take and record another reading of the light meter. Has the reading changed the way you thought it would? Wait two minutes and measure the light again. After five minutes, take another measurement of the light. Are there changes? Graph your results.

5. The result. When particles are in the air, they act like a cloud to block some of the light.

6. The conclusion. Was your hypothesis correct? When you created flour particles in the air, did the light meter register lower than it did before you stirred up the particles? After two minutes and five minutes, had the particles settled out of the air again?

You might have read that there seem to be body rhythms throughout a day. Perhaps friends or family members will help you with an experiment to show whether or not there is a daily pattern of body temperature.

Experiment 34: Body temperature patterns
Category: Health and behavioral science, grades 3–5

 Materials needed: An oral thermometer, disinfectant, and a group of willing participants.

1. The purpose of your experiment is to answer the question, "Do individuals have patterns of body temperature throughout the day?"

2. The hypothesis. If a person's temperature is taken several times a day at regular intervals, and this is repeated each day for a week, there will be a pattern of high and low temperatures with the low temperatures being in the morning and the higher temperatures in the evening.

3. The procedure. You will need to use an oral thermometer and take your temperature and that of the other subjects in your experiment several times a day. Be sure that the thermometer is sterile before each use and reads below 97 degrees before it is placed in someone's mouth.

- Avoid taking temperatures right after heavy exercise or activity. Try to keep conditions the same by always taking temperatures inside the house or the classroom to avoid extremes of heat or cold. Establish regular times in the morning, at noon, in late afternoon, and in evening for the taking of each subject's temperature.

4. Data gathering. Prepare a record card for each subject in your experiment. Include a place for the name, age, sex, date, and the times of day at which you'll be taking temperatures. Record your data accurately both as to the subject, the exact time, date, and the reading of the body temperature.

   - You will need to repeat this data-gathering process over a period of several days, preferably for a week, to establish a pattern.

5. The results. If you have enough subjects, in addition to a daily pattern for each subject, you might be able to spot differences between the temperatures of adults and children, between girls and boys, etc.

6. The conclusion. Was your hypothesis correct? Could you graph a daily pattern for each individual that was similar each day? Did most low temperatures occur in the morning and most highs in the evening? If your sample was large enough, did you distinguish others differences between adults and children or between males and females?

People have very good vision compared with the sight of most other animals. We can see in three dimensions. But it is easy to confuse our eyes. Following are three experiments in optics.

Experiment 35: Drop the bean in the cup
Category: Health and behavioral science, grades K–2

Materials needed: A small paper cup, a clean washcloth to hold over one eye, ten lima beans.

1. The purpose of your experiment is to answer the question, "Are two eyes better than one?"

2. The hypothesis. Since the use of both eyes helps one judge depth and distance, a person using two eyes will do better than using only one eye in deciding when a friend is holding a lima bean directly over a cup.

3. The procedure. Draw a chart with three columns. Label one column "Subject's name." Another column will be labeled "Using both eyes." And the third column will be labeled "Using only one eye."

4. Data gathering. Have a friend sit at a table. Place a cup on the table about 3 feet from the subject. Hold a lima bean in one hand. Move your hand toward the cup. Ask the subject to say "drop" when the subject believes your hand is in such a position that the lima bean will fall in the cup. Repeat this ten times. Record the subject's name and the number of beans that fell inside the cup.
   • Then have the subject cover one eye with a soft cloth. Repeat the process above. Record the number of beans that fell in the cup.

5. The results. The majority of your subjects will do much better using both eyes instead of one eye.

6. The conclusion. Was your hypothesis correct? Did you prove that using both eyes improves the ability to judge depth and distance?

Experiment 36:
A pin shadow on the retina of the eye
Category: Health and behavioral science, grades 4–5

Materials needed: A 4-×-6 white index card, a pin, a pencil with an eraser.

1. The purpose of your experiment is to answer the question, "When an image is right-side up on the retina, is it seen right-side up or upside down?"

2. The hypothesis. An object placed between the eye and a hole in a card held in front of the eye cannot be focused on the retina, but its shadow will be cast there, and it will appear to be upside down.

3. The procedure. Take a white index card and poke a hole in it with a straight pin. Hold the card about one inch in front of the eye and look through the pinhole at a landscape. You will see a lot through this tiny hole. Rays of light that come through the hole spread wide apart again. The lens of the eye brings these separated points of light to a focus at the back of the eye.

   • Take the straight pin and poke it firmly into the eraser of a pencil. Now slowly move the pencil until the pin, head up, comes between your eye and the card. Move the pin from chin level up to the hole you have pricked in the card. (You might need to practice a little to get just the right distance and movement.)

4. Data gathering. The shadow cast by the pinhead is right-side up on the retina. But what do you see?

5. The result. You will see the pin appear to come down into view, even though you are pushing the pin up in front of your eye. When an image is actually right-side up on the retina, we see it upside down. Our brain inverts the pictures that strike the eye, so that when the picture is actually upside down on the retina, we see it right-side up.

6. The conclusion. Was your hypothesis correct? Did the pin appear to be upside down?

Experiment 37: Looking at a man's top hat
Category: Health and behavioral science, grades 1–5

Materials needed: A drawing of a top hat, a number of subjects willing to make a guess about the hat.

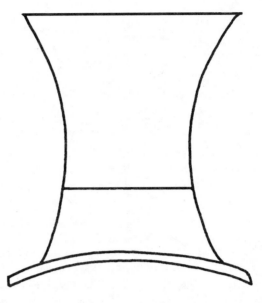

1. The purpose of your experiment is to answer the question, "Do we judge height as greater than width because of the greater effort involved in viewing height?"

2. The hypothesis. If an object is drawn so that the height and width are equal, a person viewing the drawing will guess that it is taller than it is wide because it takes more effort to move our eyes up and down to judge height than it does for us to move them from side to side to judge width.

3. The procedure. First draw a man's top hat. The brim of the hat should form a slight upward arch. The sides of the hat should have a slight curve so that the narrowest piece of the hat will be the middle of the upper piece. Be sure that these three curved lines (the brim and the two outer sides of the top) are exactly the same length.

4. Data gathering. Prepare a chart with four columns: name of subject, taller, wider, the same. Ask a variety of people to look at your drawing and to tell you whether the hat is taller, wider, or just the same height as the brim. After each person's name, check the column indicating the answer given.

5. The results. Most of your subjects will guess that the hat is taller than it is wide.

6. The conclusion. Was your hypothesis correct? Even though the height and width of the hat were the same, did most subjects guess that the hat was taller? Try other figures with your subjects, such as a simple inverted "T" or a cross with arms of equal length. What results do you get?

Experiment 38: A simple reflectoscope
Category: Health and behavioral science, grades 2–4

Materials needed: A piece of glass that does not have sharp edges (if the glass seems sharp, have an adult tape the edges of the pane before using it); some modeling clay, a flat surface, and a simple, large (6 to 9 inches) picture of a symmetrical object such as a butterfly.

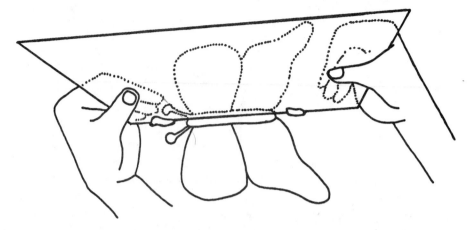

1. The purpose of your experiment is to answer the question, "Does a flat, reflecting surface produce an exact image of the object it reflects?"

2. The hypothesis. Since a flat reflecting surface produces an exact image of an object that it reflects, if I put a drawing of one-half of a butterfly on a table so that it touches an upright pane of glass, the pane will reflect an image that, if traced, will be identical to the drawing on the table.

3. The procedure. Make a simple, bold drawing of one-half of a butterfly. Your drawing should be approximately 3 inches wide and 6 to 8 inches long. Place the drawing flat on the left-hand side of a sheet of paper that is approximately 8 by 12 inches in size.
   • Put a pane of glass vertically next to the drawing and in the middle of the sheet of paper. Use lumps of modeling clay to hold the pane of glass steady and upright.

4. Data gathering. Look through the pane of glass. You will see the image of the half-butterfly reflected on the other side of the pane. Use a pencil to trace the image that you see.

5. The results. Remove the pane of glass. You will now have a complete, symmetrical drawing of a butterfly on the paper.

6. The conclusion. Was your hypothesis correct? Did you prove that a flat reflecting surface produces an image exactly like the object it reflects?

Did you know that some body functions are involuntary? The following experiment will help you explore eye blinks.

Experiment 39: In the blink of an eye
Category: Health and behavioral science, grades 2–5

Materials needed: A well-lighted room, a watch with a second hand or a stopwatch that can be set for 1 minute, a bowl of finely minced onion.

1. The purpose of your experiment is to find out whether a person blinks more frequently when something is irritating the eyes than when no irritant is present.

2. The hypothesis. A person will involuntarily blink more frequently than usual when a chopped onion is placed close enough to be an irritant to the eyes.

3. The procedure. Finely chop a whole onion into a bowl and put on a tight lid. Thoroughly wash your hands with soap so that there is no trace of onion scent left on them. Put the bowl with the chopped onion in another room.

- Ask your subject to sit quietly in a chair, close to a table, in a well-lighted room. (If the subject wears glasses, ask him or her to remove the glasses.) Tell the subject that you will be observing him or her closely for one minute. (Do not tell the subject that you will be counting eye blinks because if the subject is aware of what you are doing and thinking about it, he or she might blink more or less than usual.)
- Prepare a chart with three columns labeled: subject's name, without onion, with onion.

4. Data gathering. Ask your subject to sit in the chair next to the table. Set your stopwatch or use your watch with the second hand. Carefully count the number of times your subject blinks in one minute. Record the subject's name and the number of blinks in one minute in the appropriate columns on your chart.

- Then bring in the bowl of chopped onion. Take off the lid. Set it on the table next to your subject.
- Again observe for one minute and record the number of blinks.
- Repeat this process with each subject. Be sure to remove the bowl of onions from the room before beginning each new test. Be sure to wash your hands thoroughly so that no onion scent is on them.

5. The results. Your subjects will blink more frequently when an irritant like a onion is near them.

6. The conclusion. Was your hypothesis correct? Because onion juice comes through the air as a vapor and is an irritant to the eyes, did the subjects involuntarily blink faster to wash the eyes with tears?

One of your useful senses is your sense of touch. The following experiment is designed to show how good your sense of touch really is.

Experiment 40: Your sense of touch
Category: Health and behavioral science, grades K–5

Materials needed: Nine small circles of thick, corrugated cardboard; 18 straight pins with flat heads; a blindfold.

1. The purpose of your experiment is to determine whether or not different parts of your body are more sensitive to touch.

2. The hypothesis. Since nerves are close together in the fingertips, and since there are fewer nerves in the palm of the hand, and since nerves are spread out more in the arm, a person's sense of touch will be best in the fingertips.

3. The procedure. Find a number of adult subjects (at least a dozen) who will be willing to take part in your test. Prepare a sheet with ten columns. Head the columns: subject's name; small circle, 1 pin; small circle, 2 pins; small circle, 3 pins; medium circle, 1 pin; medium circle, 2 pins; medium circle, 3 pins; large circle, 1 pin; large circle, 2 pins; large circle, 3 pins.

   • Prepare nine cardboard pieces by using a compass to draw circles on thick cardboard. The large circles should be 3 inches in diameter. The medium-sized circles should be 1½ inches in diameter, and the smallest circles should be ½ inch across.

   • Stick three pins securely into one of the small circles. Space them evenly. Stick two pins securely into another small circle. Stick one pin securely into the third small circle. Be sure that the pinheads sticking up out of the cardboard circles are all the same height.

   • Repeat this process using pins and the medium-sized circles and again using the large circles. When finished, you will have a small, medium, and large circle each containing one pin. You will have a small, medium, and large circle each containing two pins. And you will have a small, medium, and large circle each containing three pins.

4. Data gathering. Blindfold your subject. Use the pieces of cardboard to gently press the pinhead(s) against the subject's arm, palm, and fingertip. Do not go in any particular order. Each time, ask how many pins he or she can feel. In the correct column on your chart, record the number of pins the subject feels.

5. The results: Most of your subjects will report being able to feel only one pin when your touch the arm with one, two, or three pinheads located on the smallest circle. On their fingertips, they will be able to tell whether one, two, or three pins are in the smallest circle. Subjects will probably be

able to feel two or three pinheads when the pins are scattered farther apart in the medium-sized and largest circle.

6. The conclusion. Was your hypothesis correct? Could subjects discriminate the number of pinheads best with their fingertips?

Experiment 41: Lung capacity
Category: Health and behavioral science, grades 4–5

Materials needed: An empty one-gallon jar with a cap, a large bowl, a piece of plastic tubing, antiseptic wipes, a marking pen.

1. The purpose of your experiment is to answer the question, "Does lung capacity differ depending on both size and the physical fitness of a person?"
2. The hypothesis. Since general health and physical conditioning affect lung capacity, the smallest person will not always have the smallest lung capacity.
3. The procedure. Choose willing subjects who differ in size and current physical fitness. Make a chart in which you list each subject's name, weight, height, and measurement around the chest. Give each of your subjects an alphabetical designation such as subjects A, B, C, D, E, and F.
   - Pour about 3 inches of water into a large bowl and set it on a counter top. Fill your gallon jug with water and screw on the top. Put the jug into the bowl of water. While the top of the jug is below the water in the bowl, remove the top and slip into the jug a piece of clear plastic tubing that is 3 feet long. (Be sure not to let any air into the jug while you are doing this.)
4. Data gathering. Have your subject take a big breath and hold it. Then the subject should put the end of the tube into his or her mouth and let out all the air in the lungs. Mark the water level on the jug with the letter A, to designate your first subject. Use an antiseptic wipe to clean the tubing.

- Set up the experiment again for your second subject. Record the level of water on the jug for this subject and mark it B. Continue this process for each subject.

5. The results. You might be surprised to find that the smallest person does not have the smallest lung capacity.

6. The conclusion. Was your hypothesis correct? By choosing subjects of different sizes who also differed in physical fitness, did you show that lung capacity is not totally dependent on size?

Other possible topics for investigation in health and behavioral science

➤ Do you think that one room in your house has more particulate matter floating in the air in it than others? Can you devise an experiment to test your hypothesis?

➤ Write your name with the hand that you normally do not use for writing. If you practice the signature ten times a day for a week, two weeks, a month, are there changes in the way the signature looks and the speed at which you write your name?

➤ Devise a series of tests to determine which of the various air fresheners is most effective against the smell of an onion. Would fragrant flowers placed in the room be as effective?

➤ Use a group of boys and girls in your class to see if there are differences between the sexes in how fast the pulse returns to normal after hopping on two feet for one minute.

➤ Devise an experiment showing the effect, if any, of caffeine on heart rate.

➤ Devise investigations to show what, if anything, happens to heart rate or blood pressure when there are marked changes in temperature.

➤ Use a sphygmomanometer to measure your blood pressure throughout the day to determine if there is a daily pattern to your blood pressure.

➤ Devise an experiment to show if people can tell what they are tasting if they cannot use their sense of smell and if the foods are similar in texture.

➤ Use a lead test kit to check decorated pottery cups or bowls in your home for the presence of lead.

➤ If you have a piece of pottery that tests positive for lead, carry out an investigation to show whether tea, orange juice, or other beverages are more likely to cause more lead to migrate from the walls of the cup than just plain water.

➤ Prepare an exhibit showing how the circulatory system works.

➤ Prepare an exhibit showing how the digestive system works.

➤ Prepare an exhibit showing that the heart is a type of pump.

➤ Compare the nutrients in several popular brands of cereals. How do they compare in amount of fat, calories, vitamins, etc.?

➤ Hypothesize about which areas in your home are most humid and test your hypothesis by using a sling psychrometer to measure humidity.

➤ Devise an experiment to show whether you should dust before or after you vacuum a room, and explain your results and reasoning.

➤ Plan an investigation to show whether or not touch receptors are equally distributed on the hand, arm, foot, and leg.

➤ Tests various parts of your skin to determine if they can feel things that are rough, soft, smooth, etc.

➤ Devise an experiment using ice cubes and paper clips to test for cold receptors on various parts of the skin.

➤ Devise an experiment using hot water and paper clips to test for heat receptors on various parts of the skin.

➤ Use a questionnaire to determine how many students in your class and how many of their parents always use seat belts when they ride in cars. Chart your results.

➤ If students are free to choose where they sit, observe seating preferences of boys and girls when they go into a school library or other room. Are there differences?

➤ Devise and use a survey to collect data on the effect of weather on mood.

➤ Devise a survey to be used with students and adults to determine awareness of health risks associated with a fatty diet.

➤ Make and explain a tongue taste map.

➤ Use a kit to construct a model of a human skeleton.

➤ Make an exhibit showing how the ear hears sound.

➤ Make an exhibit showing how the eye is designed to receive light.

➤ Devise an experiment about eye-hand coordination of boys and girls by using a battery and a bell and threading a wire loop through a coiled wire.

➤ Contaminated water might be filtered to help clean it. Devise an experiment to show which of several kinds of filtering materials is most effective.

➤ Locate a wood-burning chimney. Use sticky cellophane tape to collect samples from various areas outside near the chimney. Analyze what you collect to determine if wood-burning chimneys release many particulates into the air.

➤ Make a display explaining what you learn about diabetes.

➤ Investigate some common causes of allergies and the medications that are effective in controlling them.

➤ Prepare an exhibit on care of teeth and causes of cavities.

➤ Construct a simple spirometer and show how it can measure the amount of air the lungs can hold.

➤ Using a homemade spirometer, measure the difference between the amount of air the lungs of students who rate themselves as "good athletes" can hold and the amount of air the lungs of students who rate themselves as "poor athletes" can hold. Is there a difference?

➤ Design a survey to determine the awareness of health risks faced by smokers. Use your survey with students and adults. Are there differences?

Other possible topics for investigation in health and behavioral science

Selected bibliography

Amos, Janine. 1993. *Pollution.* Austin, TX: Raintree Steck-Vaughn Co.

Anderson, Bob. 1992. *Pollution: examining cause and effect relationships.* San Diego, CA: Greenhaven Press.

Bailey, Donna. 1991. *All about your heart and blood.* Austin, TX: Steck-Vaughn Co.

Bailey, Donna. 1991. *All about your lungs.* Austin, TX: Steck-Vaughn Co.

Bailey, Donna. 1991. *All about your senses.* Austin, TX: Steck-Vaughn Library.

Bailey, Donna. 1991. *All about your skin, hair, and teeth.* Austin, TX: Steck-Vaughn Co.

Berry, Jay Wilt. 1987. *Every kids' guide to nutrition and health care.* Chicago, IL: Children's Press.

Bonnet, Robert L. 1990. *Environmental science: 49 science fair projects.* Blue Ridge Summit, PA: TAB Books.

Bright, Michael. 1991. *Traffic pollution.* New York, NY: Gloucester Press.

Byles, Monica. 1994. *Experiment with senses.* Minneapolis, MN: Lerner Publications Co.

Catherall, Ed. *Exploring the human body.* Austin, TX: Raintree Steck-Vaughn.

Durrant, Amanda. 1993. *My book of gymnastics: health & movement.* New York, NY: Thomson Learning.

Edelson, Edward. 1992. *Clean air.* New York, NY: Chelsea House Publishers.

Feinberg, Brian. 1993. *The musculoskeletal system.* New York, NY: Chelsea House Publishers.

Figtree, Dale. 1992. *Eat smart: a guide to good health for kids.* Clinton, NJ: New Win Pub.

Garzino, Mary S. 1991. *Into adolescence. Fitness, health, and hygiene: a curriculum for grades 5 - 8.* Santa Cruz, CA: Network Publications.

Hermes, William J. 1993. *Substance abuse.* New York, NY: Chelsea House.

Inglis, Jane. 1993. *Fiber.* Minneapolis, MN: Carolrhoda.

Inglis, Jane. 1993. *Proteins.* Minneapolis, MN: Carolrhoda.

Kerrod, Robin. 1991. *Senses.* North Bellmore, NY: M. Cavendish.

Kittredge, Mary. 1989. *Prescription and over-the-counter drugs.,* New York, NY: Chelsea House.

Lambert, Mark. 1988. *The brain and nervous system.* Englewood Cliffs, NJ: Silver Burdett Press.

Lammert, John. 1992. *The human body.* Vero Beach, FL: Rourke Publications.

Lee, Sally. 1990. *New theories on diet and nutrition.* New York, NY: Franklin Watts.

LeMaster, Leslie Jean. 1985. *Bacteria and viruses.* Chicago, IL: Childrens Press.

Little, Marjorie. 1991. *Diabetes.* New York, NY: Chelsea House.

Lopez, Gary. 1992. *Air pollution.* Mankato, MN: Creative Education.

Lowery, Linda. 1993. *Earthwise at school: a guide to the care & feeding of your planet.* Minneapolis, MN: Carolrhoda.

McCoy, Joseph J. *How safe is our food supply?* New York, NY: Franklin Watts.

Parker, Steve. 1991. *Learning a lesson: how you see, think, and remember.* New York, NY: Franklin Watts.

Parker, Steve. 1991. *Nerves to senses.* New York, NY: Gloucester Press.

Patent, Dorothy Hinshaw. 1992. *Nutrition: what's in the food we eat.* New York, NY: Holiday House.

Peavy, Linda S. 1982. *Food, nutrition, & you.* New York, NY: Scribner.

Rowe, Julian. 1993. *Feel and touch!* Chicago, IL: Childrens Press.

Rybolt, Thomas R. 1993. *Environmental experiments about air.* Hillside, NJ: Enslow Publishers.

Rybolt, Thomas R. 1993. *Environmental experiments about life.* Hillside, NJ: Enslow Publishers.

Rybolt, Thomas R. 1993. *Environmental experiments about water.* Hillside, NJ: Enslow Publishers.

Scheer, Judith K. 1990. *Germ smart: children's activities in disease prevention.* Santa Cruz, CA: Network Publications.

Schwarzenegger, Arnold. 1993. *Arnold's fitness for kids ages 11 to 14: a guide to health, exercise, and nutrition.* New York, NY: Doubleday.

Sonnett, Sherry. 1988. *Smoking.* New York, NY: Franklin Watts.

Suzuki, David T. 1991. *Looking at senses.* New York, NY: J. Wiley.

Taylor, Ron. 1985. *Health 2000.* New York, NY: Facts on File.

Thompson, Trisha. 1989. *Maintaining good health.* New York, NY: Facts on File Publications.

Twist, Clint. 1989. *Facts on alcohol.* New York, NY: Franklin Watts.

Ward, Brian. 1991. *Diet.* New York, NY: Franklin Watts.

Ward, Brian R. 1990. *Eyes and their care.* New York, NY: Franklin Watts.

Ward, Brian R. 1990. *Skin.* New York, NY: Franklin Watts.

Ward, Brian R. 1986. *Smoking and health.* New York, NY: Franklin Watts.

Ward, Brian R. 1991. *Teeth.* New York, NY: Franklin Watts.

Other possible topics for investigation in health and behavioral science

10
Possible projects in mathematics and computer science

Not many elementary-school-aged students will want to tackle a science fair project devoted exclusively to mathematics or computer science. Most will lack sufficient expertise. But it is likely that many students will use math in the calculations related to their projects.

A few students, however, might have both experience and interest in these fields well beyond most of their contemporaries. And they might live in homes where computer experts can share time and expertise with them. One-on-one mentoring is almost essential for the elementary-aged student to experience success in math and computer investigations. Most of the experiments in this chapter will use simple mathematics. The suggested activities, however, will contain several ideas that might intrigue young computer wizards! Computers might also be used in a science fair project to prepare written reports, generate labels, help in the experiment, and assist in the analysis of the results of a mathematical problem.

If asked, most people underestimate the number of hours their television is on each week. You might want to calculate and graph the amount of time that your family television actually is in use.

Experiment 42:
How much time is our TV on?
Category: Mathematics and computer science, grades 3–5

Materials needed: An electric clock, a television set, and graph paper.

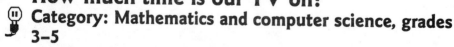

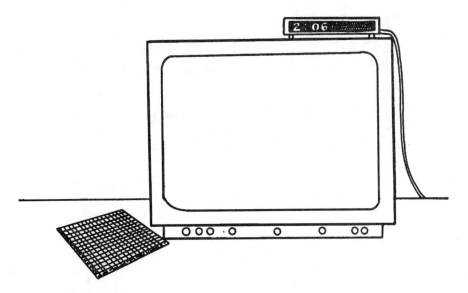

1. The purpose of your experiment is to accurately determine how long your television set is on each week.
2. The hypothesis. If accurately measured over a three-week period, the television set in my home will be on more hours a week than any household member predicts.
3. The procedure. First, ask the members of your household how many hours a week they believe the television set in your house is on. Record the opinion opposite the name of each family member.
   • Prepare a graph that will cover a three-week period. List the 21 dates along the horizontal axis. Divide the vertical axis into half hours going from 0 to 15 hours.
   • For the three-week period of your experiment, you will plug both the TV set and your electric clock into an outlet controlled by a wall switch. Every time the wall switch is turned on, your clock will start, and the TV will start.
4. Data gathering. First thing each morning, set the clock at 12 o'clock. The next morning, on your graph for that date, record how many hours and minutes the clock was on. Then reset the clock at 12 o'clock. Repeat this procedure each day for the three-week period.
5. The results. Your graph will show you the number of hours that your TV set was turned on each day. You can get an average for each week. Do you see some patterns? Can you explain the variations?
6. The conclusion. Was your hypothesis correct? Did most of your family members underestimate the number of hours a week that your TV set was on?

Although the following experiment could also be in meteorology, it is included here to show how mathematics can aid you in making and using simple scientific instruments such as a rain gauge.

Experiment 43:
Measuring the amount of water in snow
Category: Mathematics and computer science, grades 2–5

Materials needed: A clean, empty can or jar at least 8 inches deep, with an opening at least 5 inches across that has a flat bottom and a lid; a very thin dowel; a ruler divided into sixteenths of an inch.

1. The purpose of your experiment is to answer the question, "How much water is in snow?"
2. The hypothesis. Six inches of snow will contain less than 1 inch of water.
3. The procedure. Get a clean, empty can or jar. Set it outside during a snowstorm and collect 6 or more inches of snow in the can.
4. Data gathering. Take the coffee can inside and gently put a thin dowel into the snow. Lay the dowel against your ruler and measure the length of the portion that is wet with snow. Record this measurement exactly. Quickly cover the can or jar so that the moisture in the snow will not evaporate. Put the can in a cool (but well above freezing) place in your house or garage until the snow melts.

- Take off the lid and put a dry dowel stick vertically into the can. Immediately place the dowel against your ruler and measure exactly the portion that is wet.

5. The results. Compare your measurements of the number of inches of snow against the number of inches of water.

6. The conclusion. Was your hypothesis correct? Do 6 inches of snow melt into less than 1 inch of water? Sometimes you hear about snow being "wet" or "dry." If you repeat your experiment during different snow storms, do you get different results?

Lots of people enjoy eating a juicy apple. In the following experiment, you can find out how much juice an apple has by carefully weighing and graphing.

Experiment 44: The juicy apple
Category: Mathematics and computer science, grades 3–5

Materials needed: A pie pan, a juicy apple, a fine scale such as a chemical or photography scale, a fine mesh bag, a piece of graphing paper.

1. The purpose of your experiment is to find out how much "juice" an apple has.

2. The hypothesis. Apples are so juicy that if the juice were removed, the apple would lose more than half of its weight.

3. The procedure. Buy a large, fresh apple and weigh it exactly. Also weigh an aluminum pie plate. (You will be subtracting the weight of this pie plate each time you weigh and make an entry on your graph.)
   - On your graph, enter the weight of the apple along the vertical axis and the date along the horizontal axis.
   - Then cut the apple into small pieces and spread the pieces out on your aluminum pie plate. Include the seeds. Put the pie plate in a mesh bag

and hang it in a sunny spot in your yard. (The mesh bag will guard against something eating part of your apple or a part being blown away by the wind.)

4. Data gathering. Twice a week for six weeks, weigh the pie plate with the apple pieces. Subtract the weight of the pie plate before entering the date and weight on your graph.

5. The results. Your graph will show a sharp drop in the weight of the apple and then a leveling off where it seems to be thoroughly dry and is not losing any more weight or water.

6. The conclusion. Was your hypothesis correct? Was more than half of the weight of the apple in its "juice?"

A split second is a brief period of time. In the following experiment, you can find out if you can make a device to split a second exactly in half.

Experiment 45: Splitting a second
Category: Mathematics and computer science, grades 3–5.

Materials needed: String, a table, a dowel, a fishing sinker, an accurate stopwatch.

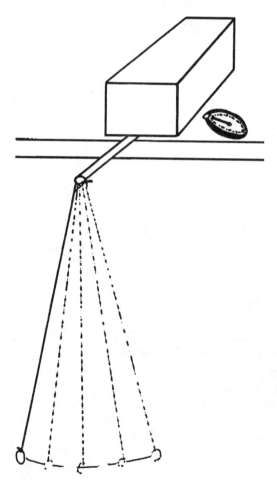

1. The purpose of your experiment is to answer the question, "Can I build a simple device to accurately split a second in half?"

2. The hypothesis. Since the string length determines the time of each swing on a pendulum, with the correct length of string, a pendulum can be built that will make a swing every half second.

3. The procedure. Tie one end of a piece of string to a dowel, and weight the dowel with a brick so that it rests on the edge of a table. Tie the other end of the string to a fishing sinker or other similar weight. The length of string dangling down should be 39 inches.

4. Data gathering. Set your pendulum in motion and time it with an accurate stopwatch that has tenths of a second. See how long the pendulum takes to make ten swings. Adjust it by changing the length of the string until it makes exactly ten swings in ten seconds. (It will not matter exactly how heavy your weight is.) When you are certain that your pendulum is accurate, making a swing every second, you are ready to change the length of the string.

5. The result. If you experiment and shorten the string, you will eventually find exactly the right length to give you a swing every one-half second. What is that length, and how does it compare with the length needed to give you one swing a second?

6. The conclusion. Was your hypothesis correct? Were you able to exactly split a second?

In the following experiment, you can compare reaction time of humans using a stopwatch to similar measurements automatically timed by a computer using a joystick.

Experiment 46: Reaction time
Category: Math and computer science, grades 3–5

Materials needed: A small track, an electric train, a stopwatch, computer attached to two joy sticks.

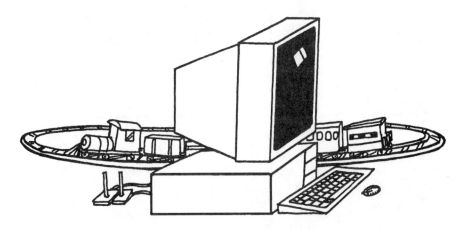

1. The purpose of your experiment is to answer the question, "Which is more reliable: a stopwatch controlled by a person or a joy-stick-controlled computer?"

2. The hypothesis. A person using a stopwatch to measure activity on an electric train track will not be as accurate as a joy-stick-activated computer timing the activity.

3. The procedure. Set up a small track and electric train in a room with a computer. The computer needs to have two joy sticks attached. Have a variety of people use a stopwatch to measure the length of time it takes for the train to make a complete circuit.

4. Data gathering. Give each subject three opportunities to measure the time it takes for a complete train circuit. Record all three of the results of each person who times this event and get an average.
   • Then mount the firing buttons of two joy sticks under the train track in such a way that the weight of the train depresses and sends a signal to a computer. When the first signal is received, the computer starts timing the train circling the track. When the second signal is received, the computer stops. Repeat this test three times and record the times.

5. The results. Using a stopwatch, did the time of one subject vary from another? In three trials, did each subject get the same time on each try? Using the joy sticks, did the computer get the same time as any of the subjects? Did the time recorded on the computer vary from one trial to another over the three trials?

6. The conclusion. Was your hypothesis correct? Was the computer more reliable than the human subjects?

Our decimal numbering system has ten digits: 0, 1, 2, 3, 4, 5, 6, 7, 8, and 9. A binary numbering system, which is used by computers, has only two digits, 0 and 1. You can use this information in the following experiment.

Experiment 47: Making a binary calculator
Category: Mathematics and computer science, grade 5

Materials needed: A pen and a piece of cardboard 8 × 8 inches square.

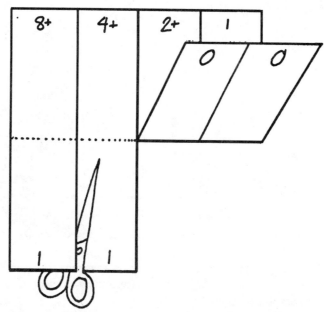

1. The purpose of your experiment is to answer the question, can a working binary calculator be made from a sheet of cardboard?

2. The hypothesis. A simple binary calculator can be made from cardboard that will accurately convert small numbers to the decimal values 0 to 15.

3. The procedure. Take an 8-inch-square piece of white cardboard. Use a ruler to draw lines to divide it vertically into four columns, each column being 2 inches wide. At the top of the first column on the left write 8 +, at the top of the second column write 4 +, at the top of the third column write 2 + and at the top of the last column write 1. At the bottom of each column, write the numeral 1.

   - Now use your ruler to draw a horizontal line across the columns to divide the cardboard in half. You will have 4 inches above and 4 inches below the horizontal line. Fold the bottom half up at the horizontal line and make a firm crease in the paper. (When the bottom half is folded up, the numbers that you have written across the top of the columns are covered.)

   - Unfold the cardboard. Cut from the bottom of the vertical column lines up to the horizontal line. You now have four flaps that will fold up and cover the top numbers. Fold these flaps up, and write a "0" at the top of each flap. (When all four flaps are folded up, you see four "0s" across the top of the cardboard.)

4. Data gathering. Practice using your binary calculator. You can fold up one or more of the flaps to create a binary number.

5. The results. If, for example, you fold up the first two flaps, you will see no numbers at the top there, but in the last two columns you will see a 2 + 1 at the top. So the binary number 0011 is equal to decimal value 3, which is the sum of adding the top visible numbers together.

6. The conclusion. Was your hypothesis correct? Can you make an accurate binary calculator using just a piece of cardboard?

The following experiment could be placed in more than one category, but it is used here as a means of employing mathematical skills.

Experiment 48: Measuring the sun's diameter
Category: Mathematics and computer science, grades 4–5

Materials needed: Piece of white cardboard approximately 8 × 11 inches, pencil, ruler, a room with a window facing the sun, large piece of heavy cardboard, 4-x-6 index card, pin, masking tape, tape measure.

1. The purpose of your experiment is to answer the question, "Can you measure the diameter of the sun without complicated scientific instruments?"

2. The hypothesis. Since you can find an unknown distance by comparing measurements of imaginary triangles, and since you know the sun is 93,000,000 miles from the earth, to calculate the sun's diameter you can make some calculations using the image cast by the sun through a pinhole.

3. The procedure. Take a piece of white cardboard, approximately 8 × 11 inches, and fold it in half to form a "tent" that will stand up. Take a ruler

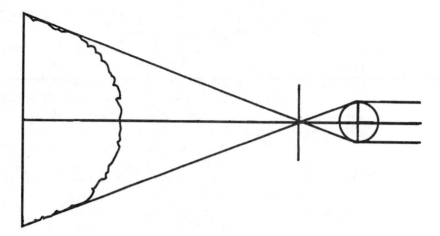

and draw two parallel lines, 1 inch apart, across the center of one side of the "tent."

- Choose a room in your house that faces the sun at the time of day that you will be experimenting. Darken the other windows in the room as completely as you can. Cut a piece of thick cardboard that will completely cover the window facing the sun. In the bottom half of your cardboard cover, cut an opening 3 × 5 inches and tape a thin, 4-x-6 white index card over the opening. With a pin, poke a pinhole in the middle of the index card. Mount the large piece of cardboard into the window.
- Set the cardboard tent on the floor or on a chair in the room so that light comes through the pinhole in the window and hits the cardboard tent. Experiment with the distance until the image of the sun that comes through the pinhole falls exactly between the two parallel lines you drew on the tent.

4. Data gathering. Measure the distance from the pinhole to the image on your "cardboard tent." Be as accurate as you can. Now you will use what you know to make some computations. You know that the sun is 93,000,000 miles from earth. You know that your parallel lines are 1 inch apart. You know how far it was from the image to the pinhole.

- You can construct some imaginary triangles with their central point at your pinhole. One imaginary line goes from the outside edge of the sun, through the pinhole, to the opposite outside edge of the image on your "tent." Another imaginary line goes from the other edge of the sun, through the pinhole, to the opposite outside edge of the image on your tent. A third imaginary line goes from the center of the sun to the center of the image of the sun on your cardboard tent. By using two of these four imaginary triangles, you can solve this problem.
- One leg of the large triangle is the unknown radius of the sun. One leg of the small triangle is the known radius of your image which is ½ inch. One leg of the largest triangle is 93,000,000 miles. One leg of the smallest triangle is the measurement of the distance of the image from the pinhole. You can express the proportion this way:

$$\frac{\text{The radius of the sun}}{93,000,000 \text{ miles}} \qquad \frac{\frac{1}{2} \text{ inch}}{\text{Inches from pinhole to image}}$$

(For easier calculations, double the ½ inch, making it 1, and double the number of inches that you measured from the pinhole to the image.

$$\frac{\text{The radius of the sun}}{\text{93,000,000 miles}} \qquad \frac{1}{\text{Twice no. of inches pinhole to image}}$$

5. The result. By cross multiplying (the radius of the sun times twice the number of inches of the distance of the pinhole to the image = 1 times 93,000,000 miles), you will be able to find the radius of the sun. The radius equals 93,000,000 miles divided by twice the number of inches you measured from the pinhole to the image. (You will then double the radius in order to find the diameter of the sun.)

6. The conclusion. Was your hypothesis correct? Could you measure the diameter of the sun from a room in your house?

Perhaps you'd like to use your math to find a measurement of an object not quite so far away as the sun. In the following experiment, you'll do just that.

Experiment 49: How high is my tree?
Category: Mathematics and computer science, grades 4–5

Materials needed: A yard stick and a tape measure.

1. The purpose of your experiment is to answer the question, "How can I find the height of a tree without climbing up and measuring it?"

2. The hypothesis. Since you can find an unknown distance by comparing measurements of imaginary triangles, and since you know both the height of a yardstick and the length of its shadow as well as the length of the shadow cast by the tree, you can use mathematical proportions to calculate the height of the tree.

3. The procedure. On a sunny day in the morning or late afternoon, go outside in the yard, playground, or park where a tree is casting a shadow. Have a friend hold up a yardstick vertical to the ground.

4. Data gathering. Measure the length of the shadow cast by the yardstick. Now measure the shadow cast by a tree.

5. The results. If you divide the length of the tree's shadow by the length of the yardstick's shadow, you will have a good estimate of the number of yards high the tree is. Multiply this number by three to get the height of the tree in feet.

6. Conclusion. Was your hypothesis correct? Could you calculate the height of a tree by using proportions of the shadows of the tree and a yardstick? (You might want to check this by using an object such as a fencepost that you can measure. Instead of a yardstick, use a ruler. How accurately did the shadows indicate the height of the fence post?)

Another interesting project lets you examine the importance of size of your sample when doing an investigation. For this, you will need a group of willing assistants and several packages of M&M candies.

Experiment 50: Sample size
Category: Mathematics and computer science, grades 4–5

Materials needed: Twenty-four packages of M&Ms.

1. The purpose of your experiment is to answer the question, how large a sample is needed to make a good guess about the number of candies and the number of candies of any one color in an M&M package?

2. The hypothesis. Using a sample of two dozen packages of M&M candies to determine the number of total candies and the number of each color of candy in a single package will yield a more reliable guess than using a sample of only six packages.

3. The procedure. Prepare a chart with room for 24 subject names, a column for total candies the subjects finds in a bag of M&Ms, and another column to record the number of each color of candy found by a subject in a package of M&Ms.

4. Data gathering. Ask subject 1 to open one bag and count the total number of candies as well as the number of candies of each color. Record the subject's name and this data on the chart.
   - Then have the next subject open a second bag of M&Ms and count the total number of candies and the number of candies of each color. Record the data on the chart.
   - Continue with subjects using bags 3, 4, 5, and 6, recording the data after opening each bag. What is the average of the number of candies and the average number of each color using your counts from all 6 bags?
   - Do you think this average will hold up if you open another 6 bags? Have subjects 7 through 12 open the contents of an M&M bag and record the results. Find the average in each of the columns for the bags opened by subjects 7 through 12.
   - Then have subjects 13 through 24 records the contents of their bags, and record the results. What is the average of this group of 12?
   - Finally, record the average of the total candies and all the colors from your investigation of the 24 bags.

5. The results. You probably found that the average of the 24 bags was different from the averages of the first 6 bags, and even of the first 12 bags that were opened.

6. The conclusion. Was your hypothesis correct? Did the larger sample yield a different average than the first 6 bags might have suggested?

Other possible topics for investigation in mathematics and computer science

➤ Explain the strategy involved in tic-tac-toe that guarantees that the first player will win or draw.

➤ Make a simple slide ruler and demonstrate how it works.

➤ Can you prove the Pythagorean theorem?

➤ Demonstrate how you can use straight lines to make a circle.

➤ Make a manual adding machine.

➤ Study Fibonacci Numbers and then use drawings and charts to show that Fibonacci Numbers occur in nature in such things as asparagus tips, the head of a sunflower, pineapple florets, and pine cones.

➤ Can you figure out and chart how to change any number from base 12 to base 5?

➤ Do a display on early time pieces and make a sand-clock timer that will accurately measure a five-minute time period.

➤ Devise an experiment to show how accurately you can measure the height of a tall or distant building by using information about the length of a known object.

➤ When you flip a coin, it will turn up heads or tails. If you flipped it 6 times, would it turn up heads 3 of those times? If you flipped it 1000 times, would heads turn up 500 times? Record the results of your sampling after 20 flips, 100 flips, 200 flips, etc. What size sample is large enough to be reasonably accurate?

➤ Make an accurate water clock or clepsydra.

➤ A puzzling mathematical exploration involves using Mobaias strips. Do some research on this topic and experiment using strips of file folders taped into circles.

➤ Set up a graphic model explaining how a computer works by showing how different input through a series of gates designed to do a simple calculation will have different effects and results.

➤ Compile a list of things that might be done to reduce computer fatigue by checking with some people who sit at computer terminals most of their working day. Make a list and offer these suggestions to another group of computer users. If they use your suggestions, ask in a month if fatigue is reduced.

➤ Design and construct a wrist pad to increase comfort in using a computer. Have a computer user try your pad and report results.

➤ If you have interference, experiment with ways to shield your home computer to reduce RF radiation. What works best?

➤ Information stored on computer floppy diskettes can be lost due to strong magnetic fields. Devise an experiment to prove this using a disk on which you have recorded a program that runs and a bar magnet that you move back and forth across the read/write window of the diskette. How close to the diskette does the magnet need to be to ruin the program?

➤ Use charts to explain how a "joy stick" works.

➤ Can you explain how the mechanism in a dot printer works?

➤ Investigate and report on the number of computers in your classmates' homes, the number of hours they are used a day, and the uses of the computers.

➤ Use computer graphics to demonstrate an optical illusion.

➤ If you hypothesize that playing spelling games on the computer will improve the performance of third graders on tests, with the teacher's cooperation, monitor the results when half the students use a computer program to create crossword puzzles out of spelling lists.

➤ Explain how a "touch sensitive" computer screen works.

➤ Can you write a computer program to "play a piece of music?"

➤ Explain how a computer can put an image on the screen.

➤ Explain how a light pen can be used to control the computer screen image.

Possible projects in mathematics and computer science

➤ Computer programs use variables and constants. Make a display to explain the difference between them and the significance of each.

➤ Construct an electric circuit to represent the computer logic function "and." Use diagrams to explain.

➤ Design and carry out an experiment using a hand-held battery-operated AM radio and a computer system to determine the area and pattern of interference.

➤ Demonstrate and explain the difference between the three basic kinds of computer files: sequential, random, and indexed.

➤ Using your computer, create a database of school volunteers for your PTA or other parent organization complete with names, addresses, and phone numbers.

➤ Choose a favorite sport such as hockey. Keep a spreadsheet on your computer of the team's games, including wins and losses. Also keep data on the weather of game days to see if it is a factor.

➤ Write a database program for a home inventory of valuables (such as jewelry, camera equipment) that would meet homeowner's insurance requirements.

➤ Write a computer program that will convert Fahrenheit temperatures into Celsius.

➤ Write a computer program that will help teach the concept of graphing.

➤ Read the weather column in your local newspaper to get your data. Then write a computer program that computes the average daily amount of rainfall and the weekly average.

➤ Write a computer program that, when you input your "earth weight," will determine your weight on other planets.

➤ Write a simple program to add two numbers together in BASIC. Write a simple game program for your computer.

➤ Write a computer program that will run through 999 numbers many times to show that in a lottery with 999 tickets, each numbered ticket has an equal chance of winning because of the uniform distribution law.

Selected bibliography

Adams, Richard C. 1987. *Science with computers*. New York, NY: Franklin Watts.

Adler, Irving. 1990. *Mathematics*. New York, NY: Doubleday.

Aten, Jenny, 1983. *Prime time math skills*. Carthage, IL: Good Apple.

American Library Association. 1990. *101 microcomputer projects to do in your library: putting your micro to work*. Chicago, IL: American Library Assn.

Anno, Masaichiro and Mitsumasa Anno. 1983. *Anno's mysterious multiplying jar*. New York, NY: Philomel Books.

Arnold, Caroline. 1984. *Measurements: fun, facts, and activities*. New York, NY: Franklin Watts.

Atelsek, Jean. 1993. *All about computers*. Emeryville, CA: Ziff-Davis Press.

Berman, Paul. 1988. *The world of numbers*. New York, NY: Marshall Cavendish.

Other possible topics for investigation in mathematics and computer science ◀

Bernstein, Bob. 1989. *Thinking numbers: math games and activities to stimulate creative thinking.* Carthage, IL: Good Apple Publications.

Bobbo, Betty and Lynn Embery. 1991. *Math around the world: math/geography enrichment activities for middle grades.* Carthage, IL: Good Apple Publications.

Bonnet, Robert L. 1990. *Computers: 49 science fair projects.* Blue Ridge Summit, PA: TAB Books.

Burns, Marilyn. 1982. *Math for smarty pants.* Boston, MA: Little, Brown.

Carlson, Edward H. 1986. *Computer kids and the amiga.* Greensboro, NC: Compute! Publications.

Catherall, Ed. 1983. *Graphs.* Chicago, IL: Childrens Press.

Coe, Rob. 1994. *Handling data: the school mathematics project.* New York, NY: Cambridge University Press.

Cote, Charles, ed. *Nimbus 6 random access measurement system applications experiments.* Washington, DC: Superintendent of Documents, US, GPO, 99 pgs.

Darling, David J. 1986. *Robots and the intelligent computer.* Minneapolis, MN: Dillon Press.

Driggs, Lorin, ed. 1985. *The Voyage of the Mimi: the books.* New York, NY: Holt, Rinehart & Winston.

Duncan, Jim. 1989. *Practical math skills: situations, strategies, solutions.* Carthage, IL: Good Apple.

Ecker, Michael. W. *Getting started in problem solving and math contests.* New York, NY: Franklin Watts.

Fekete, Irene and Jasmine Denyer. 1984. *Mathematics.* New York, NY: Facts on File.

Hewavisenti, Lakshmi. 1991. *Measuring.* New York, NY: Gloucester Press.

Hewavisenti, Lakshmi. 1991. *Problem solving.* New York, NY: Gloucester Press.

Holland, Penny. 1984. *Looking at computer programming.* New York, NY: Franklin Watts.

Jennings, Terry J. *Time.* New York, NY: Gloucester Press.

Lucas, Jerry. 1991. *Becoming a mental math wizard.* White Hall, VA: Shoe Tree Press.

Martin, Sidney and Dana McMillan. 1986. *Brain boosters.* Palo Alto, CA: Monday Morning Books.

Palumbo, Thomas J. 1989. *Measurement motivators.* Carthage, IL: Good Apple.

Pellino, John, et. al. 1987. *Discovering science on your apple II, II+, IIe, IIc and IIGS.* Blue Ridge Summit: PA, TAB Books.

Reffin-Smith, Brian. 1992. *Computers.* Tulsa, OK: EDC Publishing.

Ross, Catherine Shedrick. 1993. *Circles: fun ideas for a-round in math.* Reading, MA: Addison-Wesley.

Schulman, Elayne. 1987. *Data bases for beginners.* New York, NY: Franklin Watts.

Shalit, Nathan. 1981. *Science magic tricks.* New York, NY: Holt, Rinehart & Winston.

Sharp, Richard M. and Seymour Metzner. 1990. *The sneaky square and 113 other math activities for kids.* Blue Ridge Summit, PA: TAB Books.

Smoothey, Marion. 1993. *Number patterns.* New York, NY: Marshall Cavenidish.

Smoothey, Marion. 1993. *Numbers.* New York, NY: Marshall Cavendish.

Stanish, Bob. 1990. *Mindanderings: creative classroom approaches to thinking, writing and problem solving.* Carthage, IL: Good Apple.

Stwertka, Albert. 1987. *Recent revolutions in mathematics*. New York, NY: Franklin Watts.

Stwertka, Eve. 1985. *Make it graphic! Drawing graphs for science and social studies projects*. New York, NY: J. Messner.

Thomas, David A. 1986. *The math-computer connection*. New York, NY: Franklin Watts.

Thomas, David A. 1988. *Math projects for young scientists*. New York, NY: Franklin Watts.

Timms, Howard. 1989. *Measuring and Computing*. New York, NY: Gloucester Press.

Townsend, Charles Barry. 1986. *The world's best puzzles*. New York, NY: Sterling Publications.

Van Cleave, Janice Pratt. 1991. *Math for every kid*. New York, NY: John Wiley & Sons.

White, Laurence B. 1990. *Math-a-magic: number tricks for magicians*. Niles, IL: Albert Whitman and Co.

Wyler, Rose and Mary Elting. 1992. *Math fun with tricky lines and shapes*. New York, NY: J. Messner.

Wold, Allen L. 1984. *Computer science: projects for young scientists*. New York, NY: Franklin Watts.

Zomberg, Paul. G. 1985. *Computers*. Milwaukee: Raintree Publications.

Other possible topics for investigation in mathematics and computer science

11
Possible projects in microbiology

When you do a science fair project, you investigate something of interest to you. Often the questions that you have come from observations that you have made of things and phenomena in the world around you. In the field of microbiology, you are still observing living things. But these microbes are very tiny. You will want to look at some of these under a microscope. They provide fascinating features to study.

You might see something "growing" on a ripe orange, a piece of bread, or in spoiled milk. These are microbes, and they are all around you because they grow in water and soil as well as on plants and animals.

Safety is important in any science experiment. It is certainly an important aspect of any study in microbiology. Even though most of the microbes you might decide to grow will probably be harmless, remember that some microbes make people sick. Don't touch the microbe colonies with your hands. Try not to breathe or blow on the colonies because you could spread them in the air or get them into your mouth or nose.

If you keep the microbes you grow for very long, they will begin to smell. When you are finished with your experiment, put the things you used into a bag, seal it, and throw it away. If possible, use disposable plastic cups, pie pans, etc. so that you can throw these away and not need to sterilize them. A responsible adult should check your science fair plan before you begin. Throughout, remember to wash your hands thoroughly immediately after working on your experiment.

Because bacteria can grow in foods, many products have preservatives to slow or prevent the growth of bacteria. In the following experiment, you will investigate this.

Experiment 51: Preservatives in bread
Category: Microbiology, grades 1–4

Materials needed: Four plastic sandwich bags, four napkins, water, four slices of bread (one slice of white and one slice of wheat made with preservatives and one slice of white and wheat bread without additives).

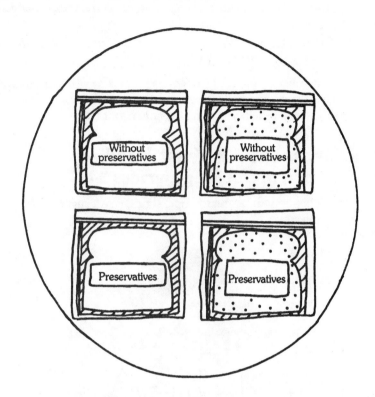

1. The purpose of your experiment is to answer the question, "Do preservatives delay the growth of bread mold?"

2. The hypothesis. Bread kept under the same conditions at room temperature without preservatives will form mold more quickly than bread in which additives are present.

3. The procedure. Go on a shopping trip to your grocery store and carefully study the bread wrappers to determine content. You will need to find a white and a wheat bread that state that there are no preservatives. And you will need to find a white and wheat bread that contain a preservative.
   - At home, mark four plastic bags with pieces of masking tape to show "preservative" on two of the bags and "without preservative" on the other two bags. Moisten four paper napkins. Put one in each of the four plastic bags.
   - Slightly moisten with water a piece of white bread and a piece of wheat bread without preservatives and put these, on top of the damp napkins, in your two plastic bags marked "without preservative." Then slightly moisten with water a piece of white bread and a piece of wheat bread that contain a preservative and put these, on top of the damp napkins, in the two bags marked "preservative." Put all four slices of sandwiched-

bagged bread on a large plate, next to one another, and put them in a warm, dark place such as a cupboard or closet.

4. Data gathering. Check your pieces of bread each day. Write down the time, date, and what you see. Make sketches if you see something interesting. Continue to do this for two weeks.

5. The results. Mold should begin growing on the bread without a preservative more quickly than it does on the bread that contains a preservative to prevent this.

6. The conclusion. Was your hypothesis correct? Did the preservative slow the growth of bread mold?

Most microbes reproduce by fission, a process by which a cell divides and forms two equal-sized new cells. Yeast reproduces by budding. The following experiment below will help you to learn more about this.

Experiment 52: Yeast budding
Category: Microbiology, grades 3–5

Materials needed: A microscope, slides, yeast, sugar, water, salt, two measuring cups.

1. The purpose of your experiment is to answer the question, "Does yeast reproduce by budding in an appropriate medium?"

2. The hypothesis. Yeast will easily reproduce by budding in a water/sugar solution, but rapid growth will not occur if salt water is used as the medium.

3. The procedure. In a measuring cup, make a mixture of a small amount of yeast, sugar, and water and let it stand at room temperature for an hour.
   • In a second cup, make a mixture of a small amount of yeast, salt and water, and let it stand at room temperature for an hour.

4. Data gathering: Place two drops of the mixture that contains sugar and water on a microscope slide, gently place the cover slip over the drops, and observe it under the microscope. Make several observations every ten minutes for an hour. Note and sketch what you see.

   • Place two drops of the mixture that contains salt and water on a microscope slide, gently place a cover slip over the drops, and observe the slide under the microscope. Make several observations every ten minutes for an hour. Note and sketch what you see.

5. The results. In the sugar/water mixture, you should be able to see yeast cells from buds that remain attached, grow larger, and that will then produce more buds. What do you see in the saltwater mixture?

6. The conclusion. Was your hypothesis correct? Did you show that yeast reproduces by budding when given an appropriate medium for growth?

Experiment 53: Fermentation of yeasts
Category: Microbiology, grades 2–4

Materials needed: Spoon, bowl, warm water, dried yeast, corn syrup, soda pop bottle, balloon.

1. The purpose of your experiment is to answer the question, "Does fermenting yeast give off carbon dioxide?"

2. The hypothesis. If fermenting yeast gives off carbon dioxide, the escaping gas will blow up a balloon secured over a pop bottle in which dried yeast, warm water, and corn syrup are mixed.

3. The procedure. Dissolve a packet of dried yeast in 75 ml of warm water. Add 125 ml of corn syrup to the yeast/water mixture and stir. Pour the mixture into a soda-pop bottle. Attach a balloon over the neck of the bottle. Put the bottle in a warm place where it will not be disturbed.

4. Data gathering. Check your pop bottle frequently. Make sketches and notes to show what you observe. In about 45 minutes you will see bubbles in the solution. The bubbles are carbon dioxide.

5. The results. The carbon dioxide will blow up your balloon.

6. The conclusion. Was your hypothesis correct? Did the fermentation of the yeast produce carbon dioxide, which blew up your balloon?

If you've ever heard the nursery rhyme, "Little Miss Muffet Sat On a Tuffet," you might have wondered about what she was eating that was called "curds and whey." The following experiment will help you understand.

Experiment 54:
Miss Muffet's curds and whey
Category: Microbiology, grades 2–5

Materials needed: Four clean baby food jars with their lids, a small amount of garden soil, a half-pint of fresh milk, a pen or marker, some masking tape.

1. The purpose of your experiment is to answer the question, "Do some of the microbes in cow's milk survive the process of pasteurization?"

2. The hypothesis. Although many of the microbes in cow's milk are killed during the process of pasteurization, some survive and will grow in nonrefrigerated milk.

3. The procedure. Using a marker and a piece of masking tape, number your four clean baby food jars 1, 2, 3, and 4. Pour an inch of ordinary whole milk into each of the four jars.
   • Screw the lid tightly on Jar #1 and put it into the refrigerator. Screw the lid tightly on Jar #2 and put it in a warm, dark place in your house, such as in the corner of a closet or cupboard. Put Jar #3 in the same warm, dark place but do not put on its lid. Add a half-teaspoon of garden soil to Jar #4, cover it tightly, and store it beside Jars #2 and #3.

4. Data gathering. After five or six days, you will want to examine your jars. As you look at and remove the lids from your jars, be careful to move

them gently so that you don't stir up the mixture inside. Write down what you see.

5. The results. Jar #1 will show the least change because cold temperatures slow the growth of microbes. Smell the milk. Does it smell sweet or sour? Jar #2 might be separated into curds and whey. The thick layer at the bottom is curd. A thin, watery layer near the top is whey. Microbes grow at warm room temperatures and change the sugar in the milk to acid. The acid causes the milk to separate into curds and whey. Smell the milk. Does it smell sweet or sour?

- Jar #3 might have a slightly larger curd at the bottom if some microbes in the air also fell into the open jar and started to grow. Smell the milk and write down what you see and smell.
- Jar #4 should have the largest curd and the strongest smell because you introduced more microbes into the milk when you added garden soil.

6. The conclusion. Was your hypothesis correct? Did microbes grow in the nonrefrigerated milk?

The air is filled with bacteria and molds. In the previous experiment, the open containers had more microbe growth than the closed containers because of additional microbes falling into the containers from the air. The following experiment will show the same process using coconuts.

Experiment 55:
Cultures of mold and bacteria in coconuts
Category: Microbiology, grades 3–5

Materials needed: A microscope, slides, two coconuts.

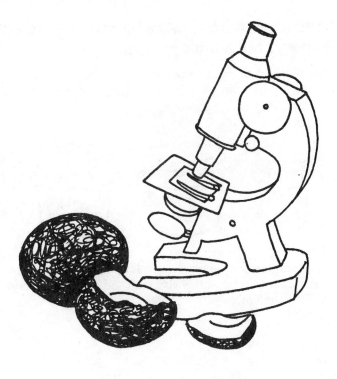

1. The purpose of your experiment will be to answer the question, "Does exposing the meat of a coconut to air increase the amount of mold and bacteria growing in it?"

2. The hypothesis. Since air contains molds and bacteria, coconut meat exposed to the air will grow more molds and bacteria than coconut meat not exposed to air.

3. The procedure. Buy two coconuts. Break one open and expose the white meat to air for an hour. Then close the coconut again so that it does not dry out.
   • Put the two coconuts in a warm, dark place, such as a cupboard and wait for five days. Then open the cracked coconut and look at the white meat. Crack open the other coconut and look at its white meat.

4. Data gathering. Using a Q-tip, dab the cultures of mold or bacteria that are growing on the cracked coconut and put some on a slide. Gently put on a cover. Then observe the slide under the microscope. Record and sketch what you see.
   • Dab another slide with a Q-tip rubbed in the meat of the freshly opened coconut and study it under the microscope. Record and sketch what you see.

5. The results. You will find many different colored cultures of mold and bacteria growing on the coconut meat that was exposed to the air. That coconut meat will be sour.

6. The conclusion. Was your hypothesis correct? Did you find more molds and bacteria on the coconut meat that was exposed than on the meat of the freshly opened coconut?

Another experiment to show how many microbes are all around us is to grow some mold and bacteria in tomato soup gardens.

Experiment 56: Tomato soup gardens
Category: Microbiology, grades 2–5

Materials needed: Four custard cups that can be boiled, tongs, four 1-foot squares of plastic wrap, a saucepan, a tablespoon, a can of tomato soup, a small tray, a magnifying glass.

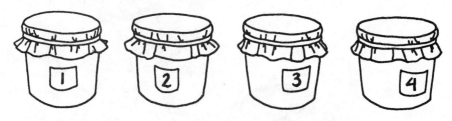

1. The purpose of your experiment is to answer the question, "Does sterilization and washing with soap and hot water cut down the number of living microbes?"

2. The hypothesis. By sterilizing and by washing with hot water and soap, the number of living microorganisms will be reduced.

3. The procedure. Place a clean tray on the counter on which you will eventually put your four custard dishes so that you can easily move them about. Open a can of tomato soup. Put it into a clean saucepan. Add a half-can of water, cover, and bring the soup to a boil. Let the soup simmer for 20 minutes.

   - In a large pan, place your four custard cups, four sheets of plastic wrap each about a foot square, kitchen tongs, and a tablespoon. Add water, cover, bring to a boil and continue boiling for twenty minutes. You are sterilizing all of your supplies.

   - Be sure to have adult supervision because you are working with boiling water and with very hot materials. Carefully remove the tongs from the hot water by using a fork and touching only the handle of the tongs. Rest the tongs across the top of a clean glass while it cools. (You do not want to contaminate it by putting it on the counter.) Wash your hands thoroughly with hot water and soap.

   - With the tongs, remove the tablespoon and put it into the saucepan of tomato soup. Use the tongs to set the four custard dishes on the tray. With the sterile tablespoon, put two spoonfuls of soup into each of the four custard cups.

   - Remove the sheets of plastic wrap from the hot water. Separate them by gently pulling at the corners. Put a sheet of sterile plastic wrap on top of Dish #1. Do not put a wrap on Dish #2, but expose it to the air for an hour. Then cover it with a plastic wrap. Rub your hand across the floor. Then stick your finger on the surface of the soup in Dish #3. Then cover it with plastic wrap.

   - Wash your hands with hot water and soap. Do not dry your hands with a towel. Touch the surface of the soup in Dish #4 with one of your "clean" fingers. Then put on the plastic wrap.

   - Use rubber bands to fasten the plastic wrap on all four of your custard dishes. Put the tray with the custard dishes into a warm, dark place.

4. Gathering data. Check the custard dishes each day, once in the morning and once at night. Note what you see. Make sketches.

5. The results. The soup that was immediately covered with plastic wrap will grow the fewest microbes because it was kept in the most sterile condition. All of the other dishes were exposed to the air, to a dirty finger, or to a "clean" finger. In these dishes, you will see molds growing on top of the soup.

6. The conclusion. Was your hypothesis correct? Did Dish #1, which was most sterile, have the least number of microorganisms growing in it, and did Dish #3, where you introduced a good supply of bacteria and molds from the floor, have the largest number of molds and bacteria growing in it?

If you have a magnifying glass available, you might want to make slides of your molds and bacteria and study them under the microscope. You are learning that growing molds lends itself to a variety of science fair projects. You might wonder what factors affect the growth of mold.

Experiment 56: Tomato soup gardens

Experiment 57:
How does temperature affect mold growth?
Category: Microbiology, grades 3–5

Materials needed: A moldy orange, a piece of bread, a piece of cheese, a sweet potato, six plastic sandwich bags, a large nail.

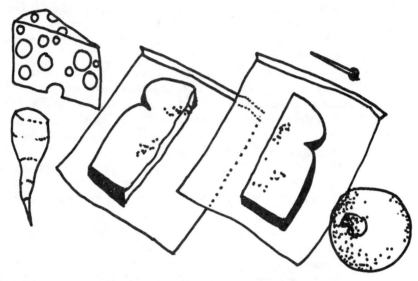

1. The purpose of your experiment is to show whether or not temperature affects the growth of mold.

2. The hypothesis. On three different kinds of food, mold will grow better and faster if the food is left for two weeks at room temperature than if the food is stored in a freezer.

3. The procedure. Dampen a piece of bread, a slice of sweet potato, and a piece of cheese. Cut each in half. Rub the tip of a large nail into a moldy orange and introduce mold spores onto both halves of the piece of bread by poking the nail into the bread and rubbing it about. Rinse the nail and then poke it into the moldy orange again and introduce the mold onto both slices of sweet potato. Rinse the nail and poke it into the moldy orange and then spread the mold onto the damp pieces of cheese.
   • Put one of the pieces of bread on which you've rubbed the mold in a plastic sandwich bag in the freezer. Put the other piece of bread into a plastic sandwich bag and place it in a warm, dry, dark place. Follow this same procedure with slices of sweet potatoes and pieces of cheese.

4. Data gathering. Check on your foods for mold growth. Record the time, date, and what you saw. You might want to make sketches. Continue doing this for two weeks.

5. The results. From your observations you can determine whether or not mold grows better and faster on one food than another. You will also be able to decide whether or not temperature affects mold growth.

6. The conclusion. Was your hypothesis correct? On each type of food, did mold grow better and faster on the unrefrigerated food than on the food you stored in the freezer?

One of the things that microbes do is to aid the recycling effort. They use dead material as food for their own growth. The following experiment will help you to see this.

Experiment 58:
Microbes and decaying grass and leaves
Category: Microbiology, grades 3–5

Materials needed: A large glass jar with a lid, fresh leaves and grass cuttings, water.

1. The purpose of your experiment is to answer the question, "Do microbes assist the process of decay?"
2. The hypothesis. Leaves and grass packed with water in a jar will be broken down into a dark brown mixture by microbes.
3. The procedure. Gather leaves and fresh grass clippings. Pack them into a large, clear, clean jar. Add a few drops of water to the top of your leaf/grass mixture. Put the top of the jar on loosely. (Be sure not to screw on the lid tightly because during this experiment gases will be given off and could cause the jar to break if the lid were sealed tightly.)
   • Put the jar in a dark, warm place. (This jar will get smelly, so choose your storage spot carefully.)
4. Data gathering: Observe your jar of leaves and clippings every day. Note the date and write down what you see.

5. The results. Over the period of a month or six weeks, you will see juices from the grass and leaves begin to collect. Microbes will grow in these juices. The liquid will become cloudy. After several weeks, you will no longer see any green grass or leaves. You will be left with a dark brown mixture. In the forest, this mixture will become part of the soil and would help to make it rich and fertile.

6. The conclusion. Was your hypothesis correct? Did the microbes break down the leaves and grass into a brown soil-like mixture?

Fences and decks around homes are constructed of wood that is slower to decay than other types of wood. You might want to do an experiment to show which woods decay fastest.

Experiment 59: Decaying wood
Category: Microbiology, grades 3–5

Materials needed: Two approximately 1-inch-square blocks of each of the following woods: cedar, redwood, pine, fir or birch; eight clean, empty baby food jars; garden soil; a gram scale.

1. The purpose of your experiment is to determine which type of wood is slowest to decay.

2. The hypothesis. Cedar and redwood will decay more slowly than blocks of pine, fir or birch.

3. The procedure. Gather small blocks of different kinds of wood. Dry your blocks of wood in the sun for a week. Weigh each block of wood and on a chart, and record its weight to the nearest gram. Be sure to permanently label four clean baby food jars with the names: cedar, redwood, pine, fir, or birch.

- Half fill each clean baby food jar with moist garden soil from your yard or from the woods. (Don't purchase sterilized soil.) Stick each block of wood in the appropriately labeled jar. Be sure that half the block of wood sticks up above the level of the dirt.
- Label four more clean empty jars: cedar, redwood, pine, fir or birch. Put a block of each of the types of wood your are investigating into the appropriately labeled jars. (These will be your controls.)
- Punch three holes in the baby food jar lids, and then screw the lids on all eight jars. Put all eight jars in a dark place and wait for eight weeks.

4. Data gathering. Check the jars often. Add the same amount of water to each jar containing soil if it appears that the soil is getting dry. Record what you see each time you examine the wooden blocks.

- After two months, clear the dirt from the blocks of wood. Dry all eight of the pieces of wood for a week. Then weigh them. Once again, record the weights of the pieces of wood from all ten jars.

5. The results. Which wood lost the greatest percentage of weight? Did the control blocks lose weight?

6. The conclusion. Was your hypothesis correct? Did both the cedar and the redwood deteriorate less than the pine, fir, or birch? Was there much difference between the weight loss of cedar and the redwood?

👥 Other possible topics for investigation in microbiology

➤ Design an experiment to investigate the fermentation rate of yeast in different foods such as corn syrup, table sugar, fruit juice, and gelatin.

➤ What chemicals are harmful to the fermentation of yeast?

➤ Compare plant growth in rich garden soil with plants raised in soil that has been sterilized by heating.

➤ Do bacterial additives to soil improve plant growth?

➤ Design an experiment to show whether one toothpaste brand is more effective than another in removing plaque from your teeth.

➤ Is one mouthwash more effective than another is eliminating plaque?

➤ Make a Winogradsky column to observe different bacteria.

➤ Devise an experiment in which you separate out magnetotactic bacteria from other kinds of bacteria.

➤ Put a covered and an uncovered container of soda pop in a warm place where it will not be disturbed. Observe. Will mold grow on one or both? Why or why not?

➤ Does mold grow more quickly in coffee or tea that has sugar in it than in coffee or tea that is without sugar? Why?

➤ Can you grow mold on leather?

➤ Devise an experiment to show that slime molds move.

- Demonstrate how grass clippings and leaves break down in a compost heap.

- Makes a display and report which molds are dangerous and cause disease.

- How could you show whether or not one antibiotic ointment was more effective than another in killing bacteria?

- Explain how pickles are made because of the activity of microbes.

- Devise an experiment to show why food that is canned might be stored for long periods of time without spoiling.

- How are microbes involved in making yogurt?

- Using a small amount of 1 to 20,000 aqueous solution of methylene blue, test milk for its bacterial count.

- Prepare an exhibit on the virus that causes measles.

- Prepare an exhibit showing how enzymes from microbes are used as stain removers in laundry detergents.

- How are microbes used in making sour cream?

- Devise an experiment to demonstrate whether one soap is more effective than others in killing bacteria on the body.

- Devise an experiment to show if one deodorant is more effective than others is killing underarm bacteria.

- Prepare an exhibit explaining how the body fights invading microbes.

- Why does yeast cause bread to rise?

- Prepare an exhibit on the industrial uses of microbes.

- Carry out an experiment to show what substances are biodegradable.

- Prepare an exhibit explaining rabies.

- Make an exhibit showing that the ingredients used to make some artificial sweeteners are produced by bacteria.

- Will an object, such as a piece of cloth, wood, or orange peel, decay more quickly if buried in one type of soil than another?

- Prepare an exhibit showing the importance of nitrogen fixation in agriculture.

- Devise an experiment to explain how meat tenderizers work.

- Will molds grow better in the light or the dark?

- Prepare an exhibit showing why teeth decay.

- Prepare an exhibit to show that microbes are grown to make vitamins such as riboflavin and vitamin C.

➤ Prepare an exhibit showing how enzymes are used to produce the soft center in chocolate-covered cherry candies.

➤ Present a display showing how your local sewage treatment plant treats waste water.

➤ The common cold is caused by a virus. Prepare an exhibit showing the cause, prevention, and treatments for common colds.

Selected bibliography

Almonte, Paul and Theresa Desmond. 1991. *The immune system.* New York, NY: Crestwood House.

Bains, Rae. 1985. *Louis Pasteur.* Mahwah, NJ: Troll Associates.

Balkwill, Frances R. 1993. *Cell wars.* Minneapolis, MN: Carolrhoda Books.

Bender, Lionel. 1991. *Around the home.* New York, NY: Gloucester Press.

Bender, Lionel. 1990. *Atoms and cells.* New York, NY: Gloucester Press.

Bender, Lionel. 1991. *Frontiers of medicine.* New York, NY: Gloucester Press.

Benziber, John. 1990. *The corpuscles meet the virus invaders.* Waterville, ME: Corpuscles InterGalactica.

Berger, Melvin. 1985. *Germs make me sick!* New York, NY: Crowell.

Birch, Beverley. 1989. *Louis Pasteur: the scientist who discovered the cause of infectious disease and invented pasteurization.* Milwaukee, WI: G. Stevens.

Bleifeld, Maurice. 1988. *Experimenting with a microscope.* New York, NY; Franklin Watts.

Canault, Nina. 1993. *Incredibly small.* New York, NY: New Discovery Books.

Challand, Helen J. 1986. *Plants without seeds.* Chicago, IL: Children's Press.

Cobb, Vicki. 1981. *Lots of rot.* New York, NY: Lippincott.

Coldrey, Jennifer. 1987. *Discovering fungi.* New York, NY: Bookwright Press.

Dashefsky, H. Steven. 1994. *Microbiology: 49 science fair projects.* Blue Ridge Summit, PA: TAB Books.

Fassler, David. 1990. *What's a virus anyway? the kids' book about AIDS.* Burlington, VT: Waterfront Books.

Gabb, Michael H. 1980. *Creatures great and small.* Minneapolis, MN: Lerner Publications.

Garvey, Helen. 1992. *The immune system: your magic doctor: a guide to the immune system for the curious of all ages.* Los Gatos, CA: Shire Press.

Hein, Karen. 1991. *AIDS: trading fears for facts: a guide for young people.* Yonkers, NY: Consumers Reports Books.

Johnson, Gaylord and Maurice Bleifeld. 1987. New York, NY: Prentice Hall Press.

Klein, Aaron E. 1980. *The complete beginner's guide to microscopes and telescopes.* Garden City, NY: Doubleday.

Knight, David C. 1981. *Viruses, life's smallest enemies.* New York, NY: W. Morrow.

Lammert, John. 1992. *Microbes.* Vero Beach, FL: Rourke Pub.

Lang, Susan S. 1992. *Invisible bugs and other creepy creatures that live with you.* New York, NY: Sterling Pub. Co.

Other possible topics for investigation in microbiology

Lavies, Bianca. 1991. *Compost critters*. New York, NY: Dutton Children's Books.

LeMaster, Leslie Jean. 1985. *Bacteria and viruses*. Chicago, IL: Children's Press.

Lovett, Sarah. 1993. *Extremely weird micro monsters*. Santa Fe, NM: J. Muir Publications.

Nardo, Don. 1991. *Germs: mysterious microorganisms*. San Diego, CA: Lucent Books.

Newton, David E. 1991. *AIDS issues: a handbook*. Hillside, NJ: Enslow Publishers.

Nourse, Alan Wedward. 1983. *Viruses*. New York, NY: Franklin Watts.

Patent, Dorothy Hinshaw. 1980. *Bacteria, how they affect other living things*. New York, NY: Holiday House.

Patent, Dorothy Hinshaw. 1983. *Germs!* New York, NY: Holiday House.

Raines, Kenneth G. 1989. *Nature projects for young scientists*. New York, NY: Franklin Watts.

Riccuiti, Edward R. 1994. *Microorganisms, the unseen world*. Woodbridge, CT: Blackbirch Press.

Rice, Judith. 1989. *Those mean, nasty, dirty, downright disgusting but . . . invisible germs*. St. Paul, Mn: Redleaf Press.

Sabin, Francene. 1985. *Microbes and bacteria*. Mahwah, NJ: Troll Associates.

Scheer, Judith K. 1990. *Germ smart: children's activities in disease prevention*. Santa Cruz, CA: Netword Publications.

Simon, Seymour. 1983. *Hidden worlds: pictures of the invisible*. New York, NY: Morrow.

Stewart, Gail. 1992. *Microscopes: bringing the unseen world into focus*. San Diego, CA: Lucent Books.

Stidworthy, John. 1990. *Simple animals*. New York, NY: Facts on File.

Stwertka, Eve. 1988. *Microscope: how to use it and enjoy it*. Englewood Cliffs, NJ: J. Messner.

Tames, Richard. 1990. *Louis Pasteur*. New York, NY: Franklin Watts.

Taylor, Kim. 1991. *Too small to see*. New York, NY: Delacorte.

Taylor, Paul D. 1990. *Fossil*. New York, NY: A. Knopf.

Tomb, Howard. 1993. *Microaliens: dazzling journeys with an electron microscope*. New York, NY: Farrar, Straus and Giroux.

Van Cleave, Janice Pratt. 1993. *Microscopes and magnifying lenses*. New York, NY: John Wiley & Sons.

Wilkin, Fred. 1993. *Microscopes and telescopes*. Chicago: Children's Press.

12
Possible projects in physical science

Elementary school science fair projects in the general category of physical science can involve many different kinds of topics in physics, chemistry, or astronomy. The emphasis in this chapter is on basic projects involving pulleys, friction, and magnetism, but a few experiments are included involving chemistry, astronomy, and sound waves. The student interested in physical science as a potential area for science fair investigation might also consider reading the chapter on engineering. These two chapters are closely related.

One possible science fair project in the general area of physics is to design a pulley to show how you can lift a heavy weight with little effort. (The pulley that you make can also be used to carry out other interesting experiments.)

 ## Experiment 60: Using a pulley
Category: Physical science, grades 2–5

 Materials needed: Marbles, an empty quart milk carton, a coat hanger, an empty spool of thread, a dowel, a piece of string.

1. The purpose of your experiment is to answer the question, "How does a pulley work to lift weights?"
2. The hypothesis. If the string on a simple pulley is pulled twice the distance that a carton full of marbles is raised, it will take only half the force usually exerted to lift the weight.
3. The procedure. Open up the flaps and rinse out a quart milk carton. Fill it with two-dozen marbles. Fold the flaps back to close the carton. Punch a hole through all layers in the center of the flaps of the milk carton. Thread a piece of string through the punched hole and knot it to form a loop.
   • Cut one arm off of a metal coat hanger. Thread an empty spool onto the other arm and bend that arm into a rectangular shape so that it goes out 2 inches from the coat hanger hook, then up 2 inches, then bent at a right angle and through the spool, and then bent at a right angle and

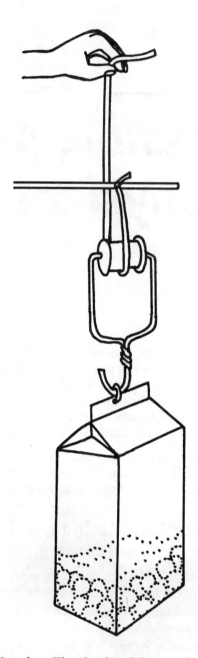

down another 2 inches. The "hook" of the coat hanger will hang down
and hold the loop that you put in the flaps of the milk carton.
- Suspend a dowel above the table on which you are working. Tie a
sturdy string to the dowel and down under the empty thread spool.)

4. Data gathering. Lift the milk carton 6 inches off the table by pulling it up
in your hands, holding onto the flap. Then lift the milk carton by pulling
the string on your pulley 12 inches. You will have lifted the milk carton 6
inches off the table.

5. The results. The milk carton of marbles will feel only half as heavy as
before. This is because by pulling the string twice the distance that you
raise the carton, you need to exert only half the force to lift it.

6. The conclusion. Was your hypothesis correct? Did the carton of marbles feel only half as heavy when you moved them by using a pulley? How far would you have to pull the string if you took it from the first pulley up over the supporting dowel and then pulled it down?

You can use the pulley that you made to do another experiment to measure frictional force. This would be a controlled experiment with one variable.

Experiment 61: Measuring frictional force
Category: Physical science, grades 3–5

Materials needed: A platform or bench about 2 feet high and 2 feet long; a cord; some thumbtacks; a wooden block; several washers; a paper clip; a variety of sheets of material with different surfaces such as waxed paper, aluminum foil, sandpaper, corrugated cardboard, a piece of corduroy or velvet cloth, and a piece of nylon or silk cloth.

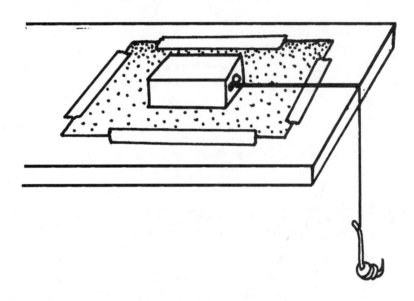

1. The purpose of your experiment is to answer the question, "Is it easier or harder to move an object over a rough surface than it is to move the same object over a smooth surface?"
2. The hypothesis. It will be easier to move a wooden block across slick surfaces than across rough surfaces because there is less friction between the block and the smooth surfaces than there is between the block and rough surfaces
3. The procedure. Divide the materials you have into two groups. One group will contain those materials that you think have a smooth surface, and the second group will contain materials that might be called rough-surfaced.
   • Fasten one of your sheets of material to the top of the bench with masking tape. Fasten one end of a cord to a wooden block by using a thumbtack. At the other end of the cord, tie a large paper clip that has been bent open to form a hook.

- Place the wooden block in the center of your bench. Let the cord with the paper clip hook on it dangle down over the end of the bench. Add washers to the paper clip, one by one, and see how many washers are needed for weight before the wooden block begins to slide across the bench. Make a note of the number of washers used.

4. Data gathering. Repeat this experiment three times, putting the block at the same starting point on the bench each time. Record the number of washers needed to move the block each time. There will probably be some slight variation. You will divide the number of washers by three to get the "average" of the number of washers needed to move the block across the surface.

   - Now change the type of surface that you fasten on top of the wooden bench beneath the block. Follow the procedures previously outlined to test the new surface. Always repeat your experiment at least three times, and if there is a difference in the number of washers needed to move the block, take the average of the your tries.
   - Try many different surfaces. Graph your results.

5. The results. When you study your graph, you will find that it took more weight (washers) to move the wooden block across the rough surfaces than the smooth ones.

6. The conclusion. Was your hypothesis correct? Was it easier to move the wooden block across the slick or smooth surfaces than across the rough ones?

You might have experimented with magnets. Perhaps you've taken a strong bar magnet and picked up a mass of nails, paper clips, etc. The following experiment is designed to show that it is not necessary for the magnet to actually touch a metal object to move it.

Experiment 62: Studying a magnetic field
Category: Physical science, grades K–3

Materials needed: A strong bar magnet, a steel paper clip, a piece of thread, a plastic berry basket, some rocks for weight, a sheet of typing paper.

1. The purpose of your experiment is to answer the question, "Does a magnet have to actually touch a metal object to affect it?"

2. The hypothesis. A magnet has a strong magnetic field that passes through a sheet of paper and the magnet does not actually have to touch a metal object to attract it.

3. The procedure. Thread a piece of sewing thread through the holes in the opposite sides of an empty berry basket to form a handle. Slip a paper clip onto the thread before you tie the knot forming the handle. Put some rocks in the berry basket for weight. Then drop the paper clip, attached to the thread, in the berry basket.

4. Data gathering. Practice using a bar magnet to attract the paper clip and cause it to stand upright in the basket. Do not actually touch the paper clip with the magnet. Can you cause the paper clip to rise out of the basket toward the magnet, still without touching the magnet? Can you get the paper clip to stand upright and pass a sheet of typing paper

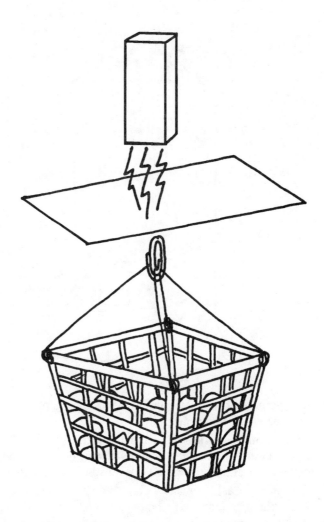

between the paper clip and the magnet through the magnetic field, while the paper clip still does not fall?

5. The results. You can demonstrate that a magnet attracts a steel paper clip even through a sheet of typing paper when the magnet does not actually touch the steel paper clip.

6. The conclusion. Was your hypothesis correct? Did you prove that a magnet has an invisible magnetic field that affects certain metal objects within the field even when the objects are not actually touching the magnet?

Now that you have studied a magnetic field, you might want to learn more about the strength of an electromagnet. This next experiment will help you to do that.

Experiment 63:
How can you make a strong electromagnet?

Category: Physical science, grades 2–5

Materials needed: Two #6 dry-cell batteries, 1½ volts; one large nail; several pieces of insulated wire; a handful of tacks; a saucer.

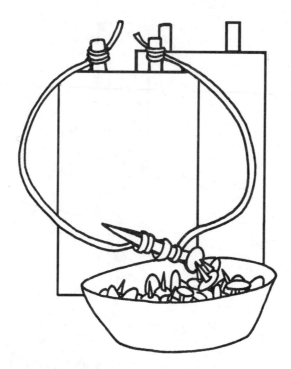

1. The purpose of your experiment is to investigate how to increase the strength of an electromagnet.

2. The hypothesis. The strength of an electromagnet can be increased both by increasing the number of turns of wire on a nail connected to the dry-cell battery and by using two dry cells in series rather than one.

3. The procedure. First make a chart on which to record your observations. Make three columns. Label one "number of turns of wire." Label the middle column "nails picked up by one dry cell." Label the third column "nails picked up by two dry cells in series."
   - Use insulated 18-gauge bell wire and a 4-inch nail. First connect a piece of wire to a pole on the battery. Next wind it clockwise around the nail, starting at the head. Count the number of turns of wire. Then connect the wire to the opposite pole of the battery. On a saucer beneath the nail head, place a pile of tacks. Use the nail head like a magnet to pick up the tacks.

4. Data gathering. Count how many turns of wire and count how many tacks the electromagnet picks up and record this on your chart. Increase the number of turns of wire by three turns each time.
   - Now repeat the process, but this time use two #6 dry-cell batteries. Run a short wire connecting a positive (+) to a negative (−) pole between the two batteries. Run a longer wire from the other pole of each battery to the nail.

5. The results. What did you learn about the strength of an electromagnet? If you have twice as many wrappings of wire around the nail, was the magnet twice as strong? If you used two batteries, was the electromagnet twice as strong with the same number of turns as one battery with that number of turns of wire?

6. The conclusion. Was your hypothesis correct? Could you increase the strength of your electromagnet by increasing the number of turns of wire? Did using two batteries make your electromagnet twice as strong?

Many science fair experiments involve using batteries. This next experiment helps you to learn more about a battery.

Experiment 64: Identifying battery poles
Category: Physical science, grades 4–5

Materials needed: A 6-volt battery, some fine copper wire, a potato.

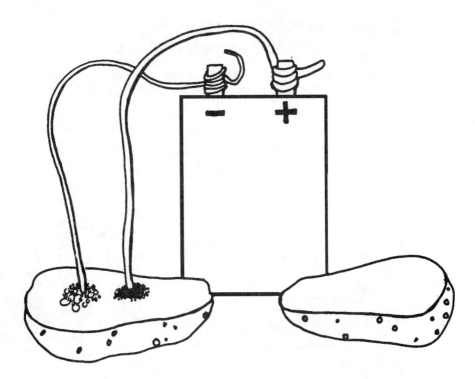

1. Your demonstration will answer the question, "Can you identify the two different poles of a battery?"
2. The hypothesis, A potato will turn green at the point that it is connected by copper wire to the positive pole of a battery because of ionization of the copper wire with the electrons from the potato juice.
3. The procedure. Attach a 12-inch length of 18-gauge copper wire to each pole of a 6-volt battery and set it on a table. Cut a potato in half lengthwise and place one of the potato halves with the cut side up on the table next to the battery. Insert the wires from the battery into the cut potato with the tips of the wires about 1 inch from one another.
4. Data gathering. Observe carefully what happens to the spot where each wire penetrates the potato. Write down what you observe.
5. The results. At one spot where the wire enters the potato you will see small bubbles. This is hydrogen that is released as electrons flow into the

144

negative pole. At the other spot (the positive pole) the potato will turn green. This is caused by the ionization of the copper wire with the electrons from the potato juice.

6. The conclusion. Was your hypothesis correct? Could you identify the positive pole of a 6-volt battery by using a potato?

You can create static charges without using a battery. Try the following experiment. You might have observed someone wearing a garment that clings to the body. We call this static cling. Does static cling occur with natural fabrics like wool and cotton or from human-made fabrics, or from both? You can do the following experiment to test different fabrics to see if they create a static charge.

Experiment 65: Static charges
Category: Physical science, grades K–3

Materials needed: Several empty margarine tubs; a very lightweight cereal such as puffed rice, salt, pepper, and scraps of different kinds of cloth.

1. The purpose of your experiment is to answer the question, "Will different fabrics create a static charge?"
2. The hypothesis. Many different fabrics (wool, nylon, cotton, silk, rayon) will create a static charge, but wool will be strongest becomes it comes from lamb's fur and contains protein.
3. The procedure. Sprinkle some salt and paper and about a dozen pieces of puffed rice cereal into an empty margarine tub. Remove the lid and empty the content onto the lid. Hold the empty container about an inch above the lid. Do any of the particles on the lid move upward due to static electricity?
4. Data gathering. Put one hand inside the tub and with the other hand, vigorously rub the outside of the tub with a piece of wool. Remove the wool and your hand from inside the tub. Place the empty tub an inch above the salt, pepper, and puffed rice. Observe and record what happens.
   • Repeat with different tubs and different types of cloth.

5. The result. When the plastic tub becomes charged by being vigorously rubbed with some materials, the puffed rice and some of the salt and pepper will be lifted up.

6. The conclusion. Was your hypothesis correct? Did wool produce the strongest charge?

Sound is another area that is studied in physical science. Wind instruments in an orchestra produce sound because of standing waves in columns of air. By building an apparatus, you can observe these standing waves.

Experiment 66: Observing standing waves
Category: Physical science, grades 4–5

Materials needed: A 2- to 3-inch-diameter speaker, a clear plastic tube, a teaspoon of very fine sawdust, a dowel stick about a foot long, a nail, a small piece of cardboard, masking tape, an audio oscillator that will produce a frequency of 600 cycles per second.

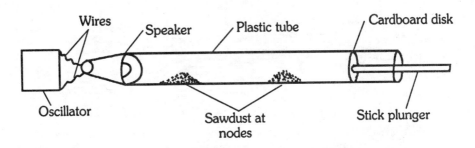

1. The purpose of your experiment is to answer the question, "Can standing waves in a column of air be observed?"

2. The hypothesis. You can produce standing waves in a column of air in a tube in such a way that it will reveal nodes where the air molecules are not moving.

3. The procedure. Place a small speaker (2 to 3 inches in diameter) into the end of a snugly fitting, clear plastic tube. Use tape to seal this end tightly. Put a teaspoon of very fine sawdust into the tube. Make a plunger for the opposite end of the tube by fastening a dowel stick with a nail to a cardboard disk that has been cut to fit snugly into the tube. When the tube is placed horizontally on a table, the plunger can be pushed in or pulled out.
   • Connect the wires of the speaker to an audio oscillator that will produce one frequency at a time.

4. Data collection. Set the oscillator at a frequency of 600 cycles per second. Move your plunger in and out of the tube until you see patterns forming in the sawdust. Record what you see.

5. The results. You will be able to see small piles of sawdust forming at two spots within the plastic tubes. The moving air molecules at the antinodes move rapidly. Those at the nodes do not move. The moving air will push very lightweight material so that it rests at the nodes.

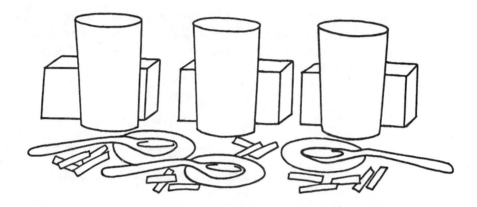

6. The conclusion. Was your hypothesis correct? Were you able to observe the presence of standing waves in columns of air?

There are many possible science fair projects involving simple chemistry. Perhaps you'd like to study acids and bases.

Experiment 67: How effective are antacids?
Category: Physical science, grades 3–5

Materials needed: Three brands of commercial antacids, three glasses, three spoons, three pieces of clean cloth, vinegar, and pH paper.

1. The purpose of your experiment is to find out which of several antacids might be most effective.
2. The hypothesis: of three commercial antacids, brands X, Y, and Z, X-brand will prove to be the most effective in neutralizing acid.
3. The procedure. Purchase three brands of commercial antacids. Pour ½ cup of vinegar into each glass. Put the minimum dosage recommended (one or two tablets) of an antacid into a piece of clean cloth and crush it with a hammer. Drop the crushed tablet into a glass of vinegar and stir.
   • Repeat this procedure with each antacid brand, using a separate cloth and a separate stirring spoon with each glass.
4. Data gathering. Wait fifteen minutes. Then dip a piece of pH paper into each glass of liquid. Note and record the color. Can you detect differences in color to suggest how much of the acid was neutralized?
   • If you do not see significant variation in the three pieces of pH paper, you will need to try some variations. If all the antacids were strong and succeeded in neutralizing the vinegar, add a tablespoonful of vinegar to each glass and stir. Test again. Continue to add vinegar, a tablespoonful at a time, until you can see differences among the three antacids.
   • If the antacids were not strong enough to neutralize the vinegar, crush up another antacid pill and add it to the solution and stir. (Be sure not to mix the antacids with each other. Add another tablet of Brand X to the first Brand X, and another tablet of Brand Y to Brand Y.) Now can you detect differences? If not, add a third antacid to each solution.

5. The results: Record what you observed about the color of the pH paper you dipped in each of the three glasses as you added more vinegar or more antacid tables. Compare the results.

6. The conclusion. Was your hypothesis correct? Did you correctly choose the most effective antacid? Was your choice made by luck, by advertising or by a study of the active ingredients?

Perhaps you'd like to do an astronomy project. Here's one involving night photography.

Experiment 68:
Night photos of the North Star
Category: Physical science, grades 4–5

Materials needed: A camera with film, a tripod, a sky-map to locate the North Star.

1. The purpose of your demonstration is to show that the constellations in the sky revolve around the North Pole.

2. The hypothesis: The constellations in the sky revolve around the North Star, and they will leave tracks of their movement in a long-term exposure photograph.

3. The procedure. You need to use a camera with a shutter that can be kept open for time exposures. There are different ways of making time exposure, and it can't be done at all with some cameras. Be sure to consult your camera manual before you begin.
   - On a clear night, go with a parent or teacher to an area where there is little light from houses and street lamps. Before you set out, load the camera with film.
   - Set the camera shutter to stay open when tripped. Set the camera on a tripod so that it will remain steady. Point the camera so that the North Star is in the middle of the view finder.

4. Data gathering. Hold a dark card in front of the lens while you open the shutter, and then move the card away. Expose the film for one hour. Then hold the card in front of the lens again before closing the shutter.

5. The results. Your developed photograph will show a series of light spots that will look like lines around one light spot (the North Star) in the center of your picture.

6. The conclusion. Was your hypothesis correct? Did your demonstration show that the constellations revolve around the North Star?

Other possible topics for investigations in physical science

➤ Using prisms, bubble makers, mirrors, vessels of water, and sunlight, show in many ways how rainbows are made. Then explain how a natural rainbow is made.

➤ Make a simple pinhole or lens camera to show how an image is produced.

➤ Make a theodolite to measure the altitude of a star and its azimuth.

➤ Make a kaleidoscope using three small hand mirrors, waxed paper, and bits of colored paper to demonstrate the principle of multiple reflection.

➤ Make a sundial.

➤ Make a periscope to show how light rays travel.

➤ Build a refracting telescope using convex lenses and cardboard tubes.

➤ Demonstrate why stars seems to "twinkle."

➤ Using a protractor, make an astrolabe to show the altitude of a star.

➤ Use a flashlight and two balls of different sizes to show how an eclipse of the sun or moon takes place.

➤ Using a chart taped to a window sill facing east, mark and show how the sun rises at different compass points at different times of the year.

➤ Show how a shadow can be used to measure an object's height by comparing the shadow cast by a flag pole or tall tree to the shadow cast by a yardstick.

➤ Demonstrate how yeast can cause bread to rise.

➤ Use a home ice-cream freezer to show that salt, added to ice, can lower the temperate well below 32 degrees Fahrenheit.

➤ Show how the sulfur from rubber unites with silver to tarnish a spoon.

➤ Design an experiment to show what affects the formation of rust.

➤ Use invisible writing done with grapefruit juice to show how heat produces a chemical change to make a new material.

➤ By making rock candy, show how sugar can be changed from sugar grains to sugar molecules to large sugar crystals.

➤ Show how a fire extinguisher works by using baking soda, vinegar, a pop bottle, and a candle.

➤ Show that temperature can cause different compounds to dissolve at different rates of speed.

➤ Experiment with ways to keep slices of apples from turning dark when exposed to air and explain what is involved.

➤ Design experiments to show how detergent added to water weakens the effect of surface tension.

➤ Find out if the temperature of water has an effect on how well detergents will remove stains.

➤ Build a ramp to launch balls horizontally and compare their speed of falling with balls dropped vertically to show that vertical and horizontal motions are independent.

➤ Experiment with the relationship between heat and color by using sunlight and black and silver cans.

➤ Design an experiment to show atmospheric pressure by using two jars of water and a siphon.

➤ Experiment with the fulcrum on a balance. Does moving the center of balance have any affect on the balance?

➤ Use a toy truck, a board placed at various angles to the floor, and a spring scale to show that the force required to support the truck is related to the angle that the board makes with the floor.

➤ Experiment with brakes and wheels by using a toy car with wheels that spin freely, an inclined board, and rubber bands to "lock" the front and/or back wheels.

➤ Design a group of experiments to demonstrate inertia, the property of all things that makes them resist change in their motion.

➤ Can the bounciness of old tennis balls be restored by heating them? Can balls bounce higher than the point from which they were dropped? Does the surface on which a ball bounced affect the height of the bounce?

➤ Design an experiment to show whether or not the weight of the rider affects the efficiency of a bicycle.

➤ Devise an experiment to show how ball bearings reduce friction in moving machines.

➤ Use a lemon to demonstrate that chemical action can cause an electrical current to flow in a closed circuit.

➤ Devise an experiment testing various solids and liquids to see how well they conduct electricity.

➤ Find out and demonstrate how the resistance of a wire is related to its length.

Other possible topics for investigations in physical science ◄

➤ Predict what will happen to the total resistance of resistors when they are wired parallel or in a series.

➤ By using a bar magnet, duplicate Faraday's experiment by generating electricity by changing the magnetic field within a coil of wire.

Selected bibliography

Apfel, Necia H. 1983. *Astronomy and planetology*. New York, NY: Franklin Watts.

Ardley, Neil. 1991. *Science book of light, The*. San Diego: Harcourt Brace Jovanovich.

Ardley, Neil. 1984. *Simple chemistry*. New York, NY: Franklin Watts.

Ardley, Neil. 1990. *Sound waves to music*. New York, NY: Gloucester Press.

Asimov, Isaac. 1990. *Projects in astronomy*. Milwaukee, WI: Gareth Stevens Pub.

Bonnet, Robert L. 1992. *Astronomy: 49 science fair projects*. Blue Ridge Summit, PA: TAB Books.

Bramwell, Martyn. 1984. *How things work*. Tulsa, OK: EDC Publishing.

Burkig, Valerie. 1986. *Photonics: the new science of light*. Hillside, NJ: Enslow Publishers.

Challand, Helen J. 1982. *Activities in the earth sciences*. Chicago, IL: Childrens Press.

Cobb, Vicki. 1985. *Chemically active!: experiments you can do at home*. New York, NY: Lippincott.

Cobb, Vicki. 1990. *Why you can't unscramble an egg?: and other not such dumb questions about matter*. New York, NY: Lodestar Books.

Conaway, Judith. 1987. *More science secrets*. Mahwah, NJ: Troll Associates.

Darling, David J. 1991. *Making light work: the science of optics*. New York, NY: Dillon Press.

Evans, David. 1992. *Make it change*. New York, NY: Dorling Kindersley.

Evans, David. 1993. *Sound & music*. New York, NY: Dorling Kindersley.

Gardner, Robert. 1990. *Famous experiments you can do*. New York, NY: Franklin Watts.

Gardner, Robert. 1986. *Ideas for science projects*. New York, NY: Franklin Watts.

Gardner, Robert. 1985. *Science around the house*. New York, NY: J. Messner.

Hecht, Jeff. 1987. *Optics, light for a neg age*. New York, NY: Scribner.

Jennings, Terry J. 1984. *Everyday chemicals*. Chicago, IL: Childrens Press.

Johnson, Mary. 1981. *Chemistry experiments*. Tulsa, OK: EDC Pub.

Kramer, Alan. 1989. *How to make a chemical volcano and other mysterious experiments*. New York, NY: Franklin Watts.

Lafferty, Peter. 1989. *Energy and light*. New York, NY: Gloucester Press.

McGrath, Susan. 1986. *Fun with physics*. Washington, DC: National Geographic Society.

Mebane, Robert C. 1992. *Adventures with atoms and molecules*. Hillside, NJ: Enslow Publishers.

Moeschl, Richard. 1989. *Exploring the sky: 100 projects for beginning astronomers*. Chicago, IL: Chicago Review Press.

Newmark, Ann. 1993. *Chemistry*. New York, NY: Dorling Kindersley.

Newton, David E. 1991. *Consumer chemistry projects for young scientists*. New York, NY: Franklin Watts.

Parker, Steve. 1990. *Chemistry*. New York, NY: Warwick Press.

Pearce, Querida Lee. 1989. *Amazing energy experiments.* New York, NY: Tor.

Penrose, Gordon. 1990. *Sensational science activities with Dr. Zed.* New York, NY: Simon and Schuster Books for Young Readers.

Stephenson, Robert. 1992. *Exploring earth in space.* Austin, TX: Raintree Steck-Vaughn.

Taylor, Barbara. 1990. *Bouncing and bending light.* New York, NY: Franklin Watts.

Taylor, Barbara. 1991. *Get it in gear!: the science of movement.* New York, NY: Random House.

Taylor, Barbara. 1990. *Machines and movement.* New York, NY: Warwick Press.

Taylor, Barbara. 1991. *Seeing is not believing!: the science of shadow and light.* New York, NY: Random House.

Taylor, Barbara. 1990. *Shadows and reflections.* New York, NY: Warwick Press.

Van Cleave, Janice Pratt. 1991. *Astronomy for every kid.* New York, NY: J. Wiley.

Van Cleave, Janice Pratt. 1989. *Chemistry for every kid: 101 easy experiments that really work.* New York, NY: J. Wiley.

Van Cleave, Janice Pratt. 1993. *200 goey, slippery, slimy, weird, and fun experiments.* New York, NY: Wiley.

Walpole, Brenda. 1988. *175 science experiments to amuse and amaze your friends.* New York, NY: Random House.

Ward, Alan. 1981. *Flight & floating.* Tulsa, OK: EDC Publishing.

Wellington, Jerry. 1993. *The super science book of space.* New York, NY: Thomson Learning.

Whyman, Kathryn. 1986. *Chemical changes.* New York, NY: Gloucester Press.

Wood, Robert W. 1989. *Physics for kids: 49 easy experiments with mechanics.* Blue Ridge Summit, PA: TAB Books.

Wood, Robert W. 1990. *Physics for kids: 49 easy experiments with optics.* Blue Ridge Summit, PA: TAB Books.

Wood, Robert W. 1990. *Physics for kids: 49 easy experiment with heat.* Blue Ridge Summit, PA: TAB Books.

Wood, Robert W. 1991. *Science for kids, 39 easy astronomy experiments.* Blue Ridge Summit, PA: TAB Books.

Wood, Robert W. 1991. *39 easy chemistry experiments.* Blue Ridge Summit, PA: TAB Books.

Wyler, Rose. 1987. *Science fun with a homemade chemistry set.* New York, NY: J. Messner.

Zubrowski, Bernie. 1981. *Messing around with baking chemistry.* Boston, MA: Little, Brown.

13
Possible projects in zoology and ethology

As mentioned earlier in this book, there are special considerations to keep in mind when doing a science fair project involving animals. Many elementary schools simply do not permit live vertebrates to be a part of science fair exhibits and projects. Some will accept projects involving invertebrates.

Before you undertake any project that includes live animals, consult with your teachers and read school or district regulations about specific requirements that might apply. You, or an adult supervisor working with you, might have to complete a detailed special form assuring, among other things, that the comfort of the animal was at all times considered throughout the experiment.

Some experiments that you might try in the broad area of zoology are about animal behavior. This usually involves activity that changes over time and might be hard to detect. Careful observation and accurate recording of your data are especially important to animal behavior experiments.

Experiment 69: Mealworms and light
Category: Zoology and ethology, grades 3–5

Materials needed: Six mealworms, a string dish cloth, a metal pie pan, large rubber band or piece of string, an empty aquarium tank.

1. The purpose of your experiment is to answer the question, "How do mealworms respond to light?"
2. The hypothesis. Mealworms will avoid light.
3. The procedure. Stretch a piece of loosely woven cloth, such as a string dish cloth, over a metal pie pan. Secure the cloth in place with a rubber band or a piece of string. Place six mealworms on top of the cloth. Set the pan in an empty aquarium in a well-lighted spot.
4. Data gathering. Observe what happens. Record the times that you looked and what you saw.

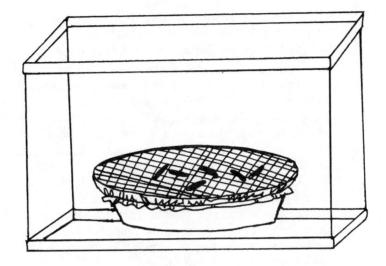

5. The results. The mealworms should move through the cloth onto the under side or to the pan below the cloth in order to avoid the light.

6. The conclusion. Was your hypothesis correct? Did the mealworms move out of the light?

 Experiment 70: Brine shrimp and light
Category: Zoology and ethology, grades 3–5

Materials needed: A vial of brine-shrimp eggs from a pet shop; a magnifying glass; ruler; pencil; a few tablespoons of coarse sea salt; two clean, wide-mouth jars; a measuring spoon and cup; a package of dry yeast; a piece of black construction paper; a flashlight.

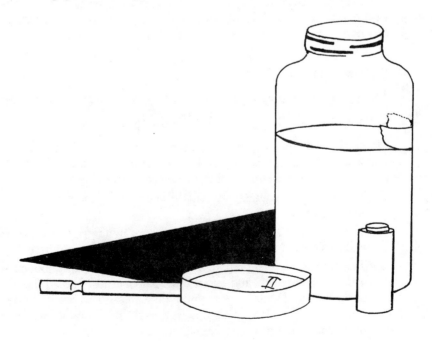

1. The purpose of your experiment will be to answer the question, "Do brine shrimp swim toward or away from the light?"

2. The hypothesis. Brine shrimp will swim toward the light.

3. The procedure. Take a large, clean jar and fill it with water. Let it stand open for two days to allow any chlorine to escape. Then add one level tablespoon of sea salt to the water and stir until the salt dissolves.

   - Into a second tall, clean jar, pour 5 inches of the salty water. Mark the level of the water with a piece of tape. Throughout your experiment, as water evaporates from the jar, continue to add salty water to keep the jar filled to the level you have marked.

   - Sprinkle a pinch of brine-shrimp eggs onto the 5 inches of salty water. Set the jar in a warm, sunny window. Observe often and note what you see. Use your magnifying glass because these shrimp are very small!

   - Once you do see shrimp in your jar, sprinkle a few grains of powdered yeast on top of the water in the jar every other day. (Be sure not to add much or the water will turn milky.)

   - When many of your shrimp have hatched and are full grown (perhaps ½ inch), you will be ready for your experiment.

   - Wrap a piece of black construction paper around the tall, thin jar. Take a flashlight and shine it directly down into the jar for three or four minutes.

4. Data gathering. Turn off the flashlight and remove the piece of black paper. Quickly observe the brine shrimp. Note down what you see.

5. The results. The brine shrimp will have moved to the top of the jar.

6. The conclusion. Was your hypothesis correct? Were the brine shrimp attracted to the bright light? If you moved your shrimp into a clear, plastic shoe box, and covered one-half of the top with red cellophane and one-half with blue, would the shrimp move to one side of the box?

Ants appear to be busy creatures that run about rapidly working hard. In this next experiment, you'll learn how fast they go and what effect temperature has on ants.

Experiment 71:
Does temperature affect the speed of ants?
Category: Zoology and ethology, grades 2–5

Materials needed: An earthen trench about 3 inches deep, 1 inch wide, and 1 foot long; 10 ants; a jar with a lid into which very tiny air holes have been punched; a stopwatch; an index card; a piece of bread.

1. The purpose of your experiment will be to see if temperature affects the speed of ants.

2. The hypothesis. Ants that have been kept in a refrigerator for 30 minutes will move more slowly than those that have not been refrigerated.

3. The procedure. First prepare a trench in the dirt that is about 1 inch wide, 3 inches deep, and 1 foot long. Rub a crust of bread the full length of the trench. Don't leave crumbs. Take an ant and put it at one end of the trench. Time it with a stopwatch to see how long it takes to get to the other end of the trench. (You can leave a crumb there if you like!)

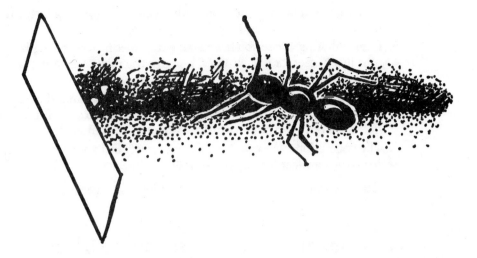

4. Data gathering. Record the length of time that it takes for the ant to go 1 foot. Repeat this process ten times using a different ant each time. Record the speed each time. (If an ant wanders up the side of the trench, gently use the index card to put the ant back in the trench again.) Add up the times and divide by ten. This will give you the average of your ants' speeds.
   • Next put your ants in a sealed container with air holes into the refrigerator. Allow the ants to cool down for 30 minutes.
   • Remove an ant from the container and time it in your trench. Repeat this with all ten ants. Record the times, and divide by ten to determine the average speed of the cold ants.
5. The results. The cold ants should, on the whole, have a slower speed than they had before they were refrigerated.
6. The conclusion. Was your hypothesis correct? Does temperature affect the speed of ants?

Experiment 72: Temperature and fruit flies
Category: Zoology and ethology, grades 2–5

 Materials needed: A fruit fly culture from a biological supply house.

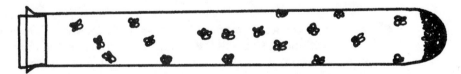

1. The purpose of your experiment is to answer the question, "Does temperature affect the activity of fruit flies?"
2. The hypothesis. Fruit flies that have been cooled down in a refrigerator will be less active than other flies that have not been refrigerated.
3. The procedure. After securing a fruit fly culture from a biological supply house, set the tube containing the fruit flies in a warm area. Observe the

tube often and makes notes about what you see happening inside the tube.

4. Data gathering. Once you have active fruit flies in your tube, place the tube in a freezer for five minutes. Remove the tube to a warm place and observe what happens.

5. The results. The sudden drop in temperature should have affected the activity of your fruit flies. What happens if you leave the culture in the freezer for only two minutes or for as long as ten minutes?

6. The conclusion. Was your hypothesis correct? Did a sudden drop in temperature affect the activity of your fruit flies?

It is possible to condition animals? The following experiment will help you learn more about this.

Experiment 73: Conditioning goldfish
Category: Zoology and ethology, grades 1–5

Materials needed: A bowl of goldfish, fish food, a spoon.

1. The purpose of your experiment is to answer the question, "Once you have conditioned a fish, will the conditioning continue for a time even if no "reward" is given?"

2. The hypothesis. Once goldfish have been conditioned to come to the surface of their bowl and expect food when a spoon is tapped against the top of the bowl, they will persist in coming to the surface every time the spoon is tapped for at least a week after food is no longer provided when the spoon is tapped.

3. The procedure. Set up a bowl with three goldfish in it. Feed the fish once a day. Each time you feed the fish, tap the top of the bowl with a spoon before you feed them. Record your observations.

- After several weeks, if you tap the rim of the bowl at each feeding time with the spoon, the fish will come to the surface of the water expecting food.

4. Data gathering. Once this procedure is well established, never provide food after tapping the spoon. Instead, feed them quietly at some time of the day with no signal from you. Once a day for a week, continue to tap the top of the bowl with a spoon and record the date and whether or not the fish come to the top.

5. The results. The goldfish will continue to come to the top of the bowl when you tap with a spoon for days after you have stopped providing food after each tapping.

6. The conclusion. Was your hypothesis correct? Did the conditioning continue to cause the fish to come even when no "reward" was given? Could you condition these goldfish to react to some new, different signal?

If you live in an area where birds are plentiful, this next experiment might prove interesting to you.

Experiment 74: Fussy feathered eaters
Category: Zoology and ethology, grades 1–5

 Materials needed: Two established bird feeders, different types of backyard birds, sunflower seeds, white millet, a standard bird identification field guide.

1. The purpose of your experiment is to answer the question, "Do different birds prefer different types of food?"

2. The hypothesis. If two bird feeders are set up near one another, one containing sunflower seeds and one containing millet, some varieties of birds will consistently visit one feeder or the other, and some birds will not visit either feeder.

3. The procedure. You will need to establish two bird feeders in your backyard. It might take two or three weeks for birds to begin to visit a feeder regularly once it has been put in place, so don't be discouraged if not many birds come the first few days. It might also be helpful to have a bird bath nearby to further encourage birds to your yard.

4. Data gathering. Once the feeders are established, keep a notebook near a window where you can observe the feeders. Look at the feeders several times a day. Use your field guide to help identify birds. Write down how many birds you see and what varieties are at each feeder. Also note down other birds that you see visiting your yard, perhaps searching for worms in the grass, but that never visit either of your bird feeders. Continue these observations over a two-month period.

5. The results. You will note that some birds, such as robins, never visit either feeder. Other birds, such as grosbeaks, will prefer sunflower seeds, while still others, such as sparrows, will eat the white millet.

6. The conclusion. Was your hypothesis correct? Were there some varieties of birds that came into your yard that didn't use the bird feeder, others that always went to the sunflowers seeds, and still others that preferred millet?

In addition to birds in your backyard, or in a nearby field, you might also find grasshoppers. These creatures are wonderful jumpers!

Experiment 75:
Grasshoppers—super jumpers!
Category: Zoology and ethology, grades 3–5

Materials needed: Two or three grasshoppers, a level area such as a large patio, a tape measure, a "bug box" or other suitable container.

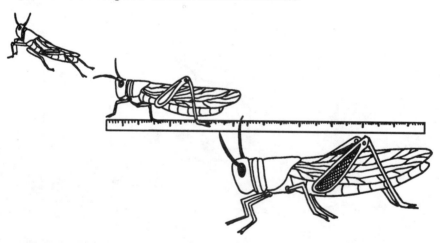

1. The purpose of your experiment is to answer the question, "How many times its own length can a grasshopper jump?"

2. The hypothesis. An ordinary grasshopper can jump many more times its own length than a champion athlete can jump his or her height.

3. The procedure. You will need to find two or three grasshoppers and keep them for a few hours or days in a suitable container such as a screened

"bug box." If you are keeping them overnight, you need to provide food, air, and water.

- Take the grasshoppers to an area where you and a friend can mark the length of a jump and then recapture the grasshopper. A large patio area might be good for this.

4. Data gathering. First measure as carefully as you can the length of a grasshopper. Measure from the tip of the head to the tip of the abdomen. Use a ruler or tape divided into 32nds of an inch. Put that grasshopper at a designated spot. Have a friend mark the spot to which the grasshopper jumps while you quickly recapture the grasshopper. Measure and record the distance. Allow each of your three grasshoppers to make several jumps and record each.

- When you are finished with your experiment, be sure to release the grasshoppers to the area where you captured them.

5. The results. Depending on the size and type of grasshoppers, you will find that they can jump many times their length. Compare this with the world recorder holder in the broad jump. (If you do not know, assume that the jumper is 6 feet tall.) How do the jumps of the grasshoppers compare with the champion? If one of your grasshoppers is twice as long as another, does it jump twice as far?

6. The conclusion. Was your hypothesis correct? Does an ordinary grasshopper jump much farther (in comparison to its length) than a champion athlete?

Do moths come to any light, or do they prefer one color to another? The following experiment will help you find out.

Experiment 76: Moths and colored lights
Category: Zoology and ethology, grades 3–5

Materials needed: A string of outdoor Christmas tree lights, blue bulbs, yellow bulbs.

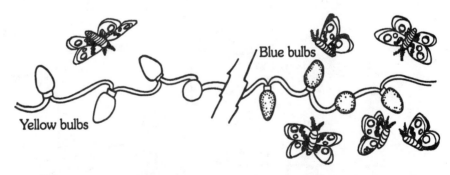

Blue bulbs

Yellow bulbs

1. The purpose of your experiment is to answer the question, "Do moths prefer one color of light to another?"
2. The hypothesis. Moths will be attracted to blue Christmas tree bulbs, but not to yellow Christmas tree bulbs.
3. The procedure. In an area where there are moths, one night after it is dark, set out a string of Christmas tree lights with blue bulbs in them and turn them on.

4. Data gathering. Wait an hour and then go out and see if there are any moths. If there are, count them. Record the time and the number of moths. Repeat this procedure for three hours.
   - The next night, repeat the procedure just described, but this time put all yellow bulbs in the string of lights. Record your data carefully each hour for three hours.
   - You should repeat this process two nights a week for a month, recording and graphing your results.
5. The results. Over all, you should find that more moths are attracted to the blue lights than to the yellow ones.
6. The conclusion. Was your hypothesis correct? Were moths attracted to one color of light more than to another?

Experiment 77: Making the "invisible" visible
Category: Zoology and ethology, grades 4–5

Materials needed: Malted milk powder, ⅛ measuring teaspoon, red food dye, a small aquarium or 2-gallon glass jar, 1 gallon of water, small glass jar with lid, hand lens, scoop, freshwater pond.

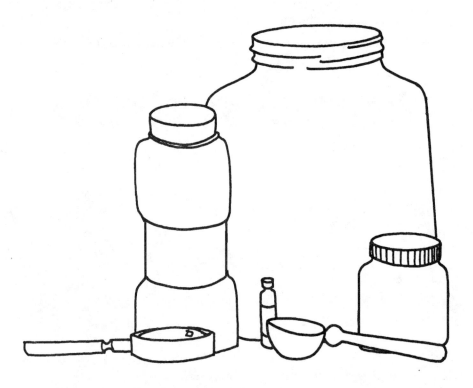

1. The purpose of your experiment is to answer the question, "Can I find a way to more easily see protozoans?"
2. The hypothesis. The many protozoans in a jar of pond water will be made more easily visible by adding coloring to the food that they eat.

3. The procedure. First you will need to take a gallon of tap water and let it stand for several days so that chlorine can evaporate. Then you need to visit a local freshwater pond. Scoop up some of the bottom debris from the pond (rotting leaves, scum, etc.) and collect this in your clean small jar. Add just enough pond water to keep the bottom debris moist.
   - Pour your standing water into the 2-gallon jar. Place the debris from the pond into the 2-gallon jar. Place the 2-gallon jar in a light area, but avoid direct sunlight.

4. Data gathering. After a day or two, your 2-gallon jar should have lots of small, one-celled animals called protozoans living in it. Use your hand lens to examine the water. Record the time and date and draw what you see.
   - Feed the protozoans ⅛ teaspoon of malted milk powder. Don't use too much or you'll pollute the water.

5. The results. Wait ten days, making an observation each day. Then add just a drop of red food coloring to another ⅛ teaspoon of malted milk powder. Feed the protozoans. Observe for another ten days.

6. The conclusion. Was your hypothesis correct? Did some of the protozoans become easier to see after eating the colored malted milk powder? (If you add too much food coloring, you will color all the water in the jar and not be able to see the protozoans. If this happens, collect as many protozoans as you can, and put them in a small jar. Wash out the 2-gallon jar. Refill it and let the water stand for two days. Then add the protozoans from your small jar.

Other possible topics for investigation in zoology and ethology

➤ Compare the anatomy of birds, mammals, and reptiles, making charts to show similarities and differences.

➤ Compare the eating preferences of a group of mice or gerbils using a variety of different seeds, fruits, and vegetables.

➤ If you construct a cardboard maze and use two hamsters, can you show that the use of food rewards has an effect on the time required to learn?

➤ Using two hamsters, can you show whether or not the length of an animal training session affects learning?

➤ Experiment with mealworms using wet and dry filter papers to show how mealworms will respond to moisture.

➤ Vary the temperature to find out how sow bugs respond to heat and cold.

➤ Grow butterflies from a culture containing larvae. Observe the various stages of development and keep careful records of your observations.

➤ Study different types of cocoons and chrysalis. Chart which kinds of moths and butterflies come from which cocoons and chrysalis.

➤ Using a culture of fruit flies in a tube, experiment to see how they respond to light by covering part of the tube.

➤ Devise an experiment in which you demonstrate whether or not fish are affected by magnetism.

➤ Do some research and then construct a funnel like the one used by Antonio Berlese. Then collect humus and rich soil and place these on your funnel to show how the funnel can be used to collect insects.

➤ Do ants prefer one kind of sugar substance to another?

➤ Establish an ant colony and try to learn how ants sleep and how they wake up.

➤ Devise an ant maze. Make some paths that lead nowhere. Make one path that leads to food. Can ants learn to choose the right trail?

➤ Gather some frog eggs. Keep them where you can observe often. Chart their growth through tadpole to adult frog.

➤ Keep a toad in a terrarium. Observe its growth, food preferences, and behaviors.

➤ Collect as many different kinds of insects as you can. Identify these.

➤ Try to find a chrysalis of a monarch butterfly. Keep the chrysalis indoors. Observe and note when the butterfly comes out.

➤ What damage is caused by insects? Find examples of some damage that they cause. Photograph the damage and make a display.

➤ If you can find a plant with aphids, collect some stems and leaves. Study the aphids with a magnifying glass. Make a display showing what you have learned.

➤ How do pill bugs respond to touch?

➤ Devise an experiment to show whether moths are attracted to heat or to light.

➤ Hypothesize that reduced habitat will result in reduced size of some animals using fish and several sizes of aquaria.

➤ Use a collection of bird nests to show that different birds instinctively build different kinds of nest.

➤ Use a heat lamp, two thermometers, and two handkerchiefs, one empty and one in which you've placed a bundle of dog or cat hair you've collected from your household pet to show how hair acts as an insulator to maintain body temperature.

➤ Investigate whether life span in different animals is related to their gestation period.

➤ Use plaster of paris to show the process by which fossil prints are preserved.

➤ Would soil collected from ant hill mounds grow taller and greener plants from seeds than would ordinary garden soil?

➤ Study and explain how earthworms reproduce.

➤ How do earthworms respond to water?

➤ What do earthworms do to the soil?

➤ Devise an experiment to show whether or not earthworms can learn.

➤ If you place a pan of sugar water in your backyard at ground level, what creatures will drink from it by day? By night?

Possible projects in zoology and ethology

> If you put pans of water, sugar water, soda pop, or honey/water mixture in an area where there are insects, which pan will be the favorite of which insects?

> Make frequent observations of several spiderwebs to find out if larger webs are made by larger spiders and if larger webs catch more food.

> Make a display showing different types of spiderwebs.

> Devise an experiment using different sized pieces of plywood left undisturbed on patches of soil for two weeks to hypothesize about the relationship between habitat size and the number of organisms such as worms, grubs, centipedes, etc. living there.

> Some caterpillars are strangely marked. They might look like monsters to frighten away their enemies. Examples are puss-moth larvae and the spicebush swallowtail butterfly larva. Make an exhibit showing how their markings look.

> Some animals change their metabolism in the winter and become less active. With adult supervision, attach a thermometer to a broom handle and test your hypothesis about what the temperature of the soil underneath a lake will be when the surface of the lake is frozen.

> Devise an experiment in which you use lard (similar to the fat of seals, walruses, and whales) to show that mammals that live in the sea maintain their warm temperatures by their insulating fat.

Selected bibliography

Bell, William J. 1981. *The laboratory cockroach: experiments in cockroach anatomy, physiology, and behaviour.* New York, NY: Chapman and Hall.

Berman, Paul and Keith Wicks. 1988. *The living world.* New York, NY: Marshall Cavendish.

Bonnet, Robert L. 1990. *Environmental science: 49 science fair projects.* Blue Ridge Summit, PA: TAB Books.

Boyston, Angela. 1989. *The frog. New York, NY: Warwick Press.*

Broekel, Ray. 1990. *Animal observations.* Chicago, IL: Children's Press.

Buller, Laura and Ron Taylor. 1990. *Habitats and environments. New York, NY: M. Cavendish Corporation.*

Burton, Jane. 1992. *Chick.* New York, NY: Lodestar Books.

Cherfas, Jeremy. 1991. *Animal builders.* Minneapolis, MN: Lerner Publications.

Dashefsky, H. Steve. 1992. *Insect biology: 49 science fair projects.* Blue Ridge Summit, PA: TAB Books.

Doris, Ellen. 1993. *Entomology.* New York, NY: Thames & Hudson.

Doris, Ellen. 1993. *Invertebrate zoology.* New York, NY: Thames & Hudson.

Dykstra, Mary. 1994. *The amateur zoologist: explorations and investigations.* New York, NY: Franklin Watts.

Feltwell, John. 1988. *Animals and where they live.* New York, NY: Grosset & Dunlap, Inc.

Gardner, Robert. 1992. *Robert Gardner's favorite science experiments.* New York, NY: Franklin Watts.

Other possible topics for investigation in zoology and ethology

Glaser, Linda. 1992. *Wonderful worms*. Brookfield, CT: Millbrook Press.

Goodman, Billy. 1991. *Animal homes and societies*. Boston, MA: Little, Brown.

Grant, Lesley. 1991. *Discover bones: explore the science of skeletons*. Reading, MA: Addison-Wesley Pub. Co.

Harrison, Virginia. 1990. *The world of animals*. Milwaukee, WI: Gareth Stevens Children's Books.

Hickman, Pamela M. 1993. *Habitats: making homes for animals and plants*. Reading, MA: Addison-Wesley Pub. Co.

Horner, John R. 1992. *Digging up tyrannosaurus rex*. New York, NY: Crown.

Hughey, Pat. 1984. *Scavengers and decomposers: the cleanup crew*. New York, NY: Atheneum.

Ingram, Jay. 1992. *Real live science*. Toronto: Greey de Pencier.

Johnson, Rolf E. 1992. *Dinosaur hunt!* Milwaukee, WI: Gareth Stevens Publ.

Kidlinski, Kathleen V. 1991. *Animal tracks and traces*. New York, NY: Franklin Watts.

Kneidel, Sally Stenhouse. 1993. *Creepy crawlies and the scientific method: over 100 hands-on science experiments for children*. Golden, CO: Fulcrum Publishing.

Morris, Desmond. 1990. *Animal watching*. New York, NY: Crown Publishers.

Norsgaard, E. Jaediker. 1988. *How to raise butterflies*. New York, NY: Dodd, Mead.

Parker, Steve. 1993. *Prehistoric life*. New York, NY: Dorling Kindersley.

Pearce, Querida Lee. 1992. *Why is a frog not a toad?: discovering the differences between animal look-alikes*. Chicago, IL: Contemporary Books.

Pope, Joyce. 1986. *Do animals dream? Children's questions about animals most often asked of the natural history museum*. New York, NY: Viking Kestrel.

Porter, Keith. 1987. *How animals behave*. New York, NY: Facts on File.

Roop, Peter. 1992. *One earth, a multitude of creatures*. New York, NY: Walker.

Rowan, James P. 1993. *Ants*. Vero Beach, FL: Rourke Corporation.

Settel, Joanne. 1986. *How do ants know when you're having a picnic?: (and other questions kids ask about crawly things)*. New York, NY: Atheneum.

Schlein, Miriam. 1991. *Let's go dinosaur tracing!* New York, NY: HarperCollins.

Shedd, Warner. 1994. *The kids' wildlife book*. Charlotte, VT: Williamson Pub.

Silver, Donald M. 1987. *The animal world*. New York, NY: Random House.

Slater, Peter James Bramwell. 1985. *An introduction to ethology*. New York, NY: Cambridge University Press.

Tant, Carl. 1992. *Science fair spelled w-i-n: a guide for parents, teachers, and students*. Angleton, TX: Biotech Pub.

Taylor, Kim. 1990. *Hidden underneath*. New York, NY: Delacorte Press.

Taylor, Kim. 1992. *Structure*. New York, NY: John Wiley.

Time-Life Books, eds. 1992. *Animal Behavior*. Alexandria, VA: Time-Life.

Tison, Annette. 1987. *The big book of amazing animal behavior*. New York, NY: Grosset and Dunlap, Inc.

Tocci, Salvatore. 1987. *Biology projects for young scientists*. New York, NY: Franklin Watts.

Van Cleave, Janice Pratt. 1993. *Janice Van Cleave's animals*. New York, NY: John Wiley.

Possible projects in zoology and ethology

Whalley, Paul Ernest Sutton. 1988. *Butterfly and moth*. New York, NY: Knopf.

Whitfield, Philip. 1992. *MacMillan children's guide to dinosaurs and other prehistoric animals*. New York, NY: Macmillan Pub. Co.

Wong, Ovid K. 1988. *Experiments with animal behavior*. Chicago, IL: Childrens Press.

Wood, Robert W. 1991. *Science for kids: 39 easy animal biology experiments*. Blue Ridge Summit, PA: TAB Books.

14

Exhibiting and judging at the fair

Whether it's the first time or the tenth time that it's been held, the week of the elementary school science fair might be a little chaotic. Good preplanning can avoid some of this. But a little chaos simply has to be expected and accepted.

No matter how hard a science fair committee plans, and especially if it's a first-time event, a few things will go wrong. Recognizing this in advance, realizing that it's a learning experience for all, and maintaining a good sense of humor will see everyone through. Building in a process for evaluation will guarantee some suggestions that will make the next fair even better.

Publicity

It's been suggested elsewhere in this book that the science fair should be listed on the school yearly calendar of events and that there be short articles about the fair throughout the year in the school newsletter. The newsletter is also an excellent place to advertise for needed judges and mentors for students.

The hope is that all year long, teachers have been communicating information about the fair with parents. (See chapter 2, "The teacher's role in the elementary school science fair.") And if this has been going on, most of the parents connected with the school are well aware of the fair.

But publicity can go well beyond the school. A science fair is also an excellent way to showcase the work of students before the school neighborhood and the community as a whole. Perhaps one science fair committee member will tackle such publicity. It might mean calling up (well in advance) the editor of a neighborhood newsletter to include an article and the times and dates of the fair, along with an invitation to attend. The superintendent, members of the board of education, science resource teachers, etc. also need an invitation.

Newspaper publicity is hard to come by, but it's worth a try. Often a school news reporter will be willing to write an article and include a picture of a project in progress along with the dates of the fair if you can come up with some interesting angle. If, for example, one of the projects being prepared for the fair directly relates to some current community issue, you might entice the newspaper to run an article and a photo showing the mayor consulting with the student.

In school newsletters in the weeks just before the fair, an open invitation to all parents to attend should be given. And a few days before the fair, perhaps a special flyer could be sent home as yet one more reminder.

Registration of projects

It's important to know how many exhibits the science fair committee can expect. Even with preregistration, the number of entrants will only be approximate. On the day of the fair, some students will be absent, and their exhibits will be missing. And some students who forgot to register will suddenly appear with a fair entry. The committee needs to be as flexible as possible and try to take such events in stride.

Use a registration form similar to the one shown on page 168, and have the due date for receipt of this form at least three weeks prior to the fair. The science fair committee needs sufficient time to meet and go through the registration forms, divide them into the various categories of exhibits, give each an entry number, make a master sheet of exhibitors that lists student name along with title of exhibit, name of classroom teacher, entry number, and category number.

Committee members also need to realize that some stragglers will come in after the due date. Some registration forms will even turn up on the day of the fair. If possible, accept these late entries. While rules and deadlines are important,

ELEMENTARY SCHOOL SCIENCE FAIR
REGISTRATION

Student name(s): _____

_____

_____

Grade: _____ Teacher: _____

Category of Project: _____

Title of Project: _____

_____

Special Needs: Electrical outlet: Yes _____ No _____
(If electricity is used, the student
is responsible for providing a 25-ft. extension
cord.)

                  Other:

Size of free-standing student display board when set up:

Height: _____   (5.5 feet maximum allowed)

Side to Side: _____   (4.0 feet maximum allowed)

Depth, front to back: _____   (2.5 feet maximum allowed)

I have discussed the purpose and procedures of the school science fair with
this student.

Teacher's Signature: _____

I have read the school science fair guidelines, and my child has my
permission to enter the school science fair.

Parent's Signature: _____

Date: _____

The deadline for submitting this registration
to a member of the school science fair committee is:

_____
(date)

of even greater importance is the improved self-esteem that results from the participation of eager elementary students.

Awards, time, space, and personnel needs

From the master sheet of registrations, the science fair committee next needs to make up a set of category sheets that list all of the entries in each display category. The categories might vary from school to school and district to district. The ones suggested in this book are: botany, earth science and geography, engineering, health and behavioral science, mathematics and computer science, microbiology, physical science, and zoology.

This category information is needed to assure that enough table space is available to hold the number of entries in each broad section and to be certain that enough judges are available to consult with students who have projects in each category.

Using these category sheets, the science fair committee can make a floor plan of the gym or other space where the fair is to be held. Indicate on the floor plan where and how many tables will be set to house the exhibits, and list each exhibit by registration number onto the floor plan.

If, for example, in the category of botany, the committee finds that it has 36 entries and knows that 4 entries will fit back-to-back on a single display table, the committee will designate 10 tables for botany exhibits. They'll log in the 36 entry numbers on 9 tables and have 1 extra table ready to accommodate any stragglers who appear.

After going through this process with every category, the science fair committee will have detailed sheets for each category and know how many entries to expect, how many tables are needed, where the tables will be set up the day of the fair, and where each exhibit will be placed.

Science fair certificate

For each entry in the fair, science fair committee members will complete a certificate. These certificates can be purchased from school supply companies, can be made using computer programs, or can be run off on copy machines. A typical one is shown on page 170, and a completed one is shown on page 171.

A participant's ribbon can be stapled to one corner of the certificate. (If it is a joint entry, be sure that there are two ribbons and two certificates. If an entire kindergarten class enters one class exhibit, paper-clip a ribbon for each class member to the certificate.) Participants' ribbons can be made locally or ordered quite inexpensively from a school supply catalogue.

Be sure to order a sufficient number of both certificates and ribbons well in advance of the fair. Except for the judges' comments, these certificates should be filled out as soon after registration as possible and kept in bundles by categories.

If the science fair committee is also going to award a dozen certificates of merit or distribute some special ribbons or awards for projects designated to go on to district competition, or for some other type of recognition, additional certificates or ribbons designating these special awards should be on hand.

Science Fair Certificate of

ACHIEVEMENT

Presented to _____

School _____

Category _____

Project _____

Comments _____

_____

Signature _____

Date _____

Science Fair Certificate of
ACHIEVEMENT

Presented to _____ *Katherine Stefanski* _____

School _____ *J. A. Allard Elementary* _____

Category _____ *Computer science* _____

Project _____ *"Outwitting your computer"* _____

Comments _____ *The most innovative project here,* _____

_____ *possibly a future Nobel prize winner.* _____

_____

_____ *Albert Einstein* _____ *November 5, 1994* _____
Signature · Date

A timetable needs to be created for carrying out the fair. The amount of time needed depends on the size of the school, the number of committee members, and the number of fair entries. In some cases, the setup, judging, visiting of the fair during the day by classrooms, the evening display, and the take-down can all occur in one day. In other cases, the setup and the viewing by students in all classrooms of projects in the fair will take place on one day, with the judging and public open house for the fair held on the following day.

At some point, depending on the time schedule worked out, the tables will need to be set up in the display area. Custodians, teachers, and parents need to be out in force to help with this. (If the tables are coming from classrooms, they needed to be pushed out into the halls and the homeroom number to which each table should be returned should be taped onto the bottom of each table.) If the tables are being brought out to the school from a central source, just to be used for the fair, they need to be ordered well in advance so that delivery is timely.

Big banners along the walls or hanging overhead should indicate the various sections of the gym where each category will be housed. It might be possible to run off handsome banners using a computer program, or, using magic markers, the categories can be written on posters in large letters.

On the day of the fair, a parent and a teacher from the science fair committee should plan to spend the entire day at the fair. A substitute should be used to free up the teacher for the day. These duties cannot be worked in around class-room teaching. Others might help as their time permits, but these two committee members will help maintain order and consistency throughout the fair.

Freestanding display boards

A detailed description of a free-standing display board is shown in chapter 1. To suit your school needs, the dimensions that your science fair committee decides upon might vary from the example. Even though your directions have been clear, there will probably be some exhibits that reach the committee that are "free-falling display boards." Be prepared for this.

On the day of the fair, science fair committee members should have available scissors, string, and several rolls of masking tape. Some extra sheets of cardboard and a marking pen will also come in handy. A little last-minute adjustment for some of the project displays is almost certain to be needed.

It will be a committee decision as to what to do with those projects that do not meet the specified dimensions for display. Can the project that's too tall be accommodated by setting it on the floor? Can the tiny one simply be put in its place? Whenever possible at the elementary building level, opt for flexibility. If projects are going on to a district competition, students will need to be advised that little or no leeway from standards can be tolerated at that level.

The two members of the science fair committee can arrange to have a class of students bring its exhibits to the gym and, by consulting the master floor plan, can direct each student to the table where he or she should put up the exhibit. The amount of time needed for this class of students to do this will vary according to the number of entries in the fair and the age of the students. At the same time that exhibits are being set up, the certificates (completed except for the judges comments and signature) with a participant ribbon already stapled to them should be paper-clipped to the display boards.

Now, with exhibits in place, ribbons and certificates attached, and banners indicating the various categories of the display, the fair is indeed a colorful delight to behold!

Safety considerations

Safety considerations should be given priority at all stages of the fair. In chapters 1, 2, and 3, these safety measures have been stressed. But it is important to keep them in mind again as the fair is set up.

Be certain that extension cords are not stretched across an area in such a way that they might trip people. Be alert to glass containers that might easily break. The last thing you want is for someone to be hurt at the fair.

Judges' work sheets

The important thing to remember about judging at the elementary school science fair is that judges write some supportive statements on the certificate attached to each exhibit. A judge might write a short comment like the following. "You collected plenty of data to convince me that your hypothesis was correct, and you did a good job of sharing your data through a well-constructed graph as well as in a clearly written report."

Such comments acknowledge some of the things that the student has done well and are evidence that the judge has spent some time looking at and thinking about the student's work. If a more formal evaluation is needed, or if a small number of the projects are going to be selected to be sent on to further competition at the district level, a work sheet such as the one on page 174 might be used. This sheet could be retained by the judge and used to assess and pick a small number of outstanding projects, or it could be handed to the student during the personal interview with the student.

Interviews with young scientists

At many elementary school science fairs, sufficient judges are found so that a judge need look at only four to six projects during an hour. In that time, the judge makes a comment on the certificate, completes a "judging evaluation sheet" described previously, and also holds a short, personal interview with the student.

An effective technique on the day of the fair is to assign a "runner" to each judge. The runners can be students selected by the science fair committee to assist on fair day. Referring to the judge's list of entries to be judged (which includes project name and number, student name, and name of student's teacher), the runner can leave the display hall and go to the appropriate classroom to get the student(s).

The judge can then talk to the student about his or her project, asking questions, offering observations and suggestions, and giving positive feedback to the project. It's a great opportunity for a student to explain orally how the project was carried out and even to ask a few questions.

Judges' evaluation sheet

Since written comments (on the science fair certificate or on the judging evaluation sheet) are necessarily brief, the addition of a personal interview adds a great deal to the evaluation process. Students might be nervous, and judges should be encouraged to set the young scientists at ease. The figure on page 176 shows how those who attend the fair might make comments.

Quality of displayed print materials

One area that might come up for discussion during the interviews is the quality of displayed print materials. Comments might certainly be made about the neatness of the lettering and accuracy of spelling. But perhaps more importantly, this is an opportunity to talk about the variety of ways in which results of the project might be displayed.

If the student simply wrote a paragraph describing the results and findings, this is an opportunity for a judge to suggest that a chart or graph might be a valuable addition. And it's also a time to emphasize that using mathematics can enhance the project. For example, instead of saying that the "average time was 41 seconds," the science fair project gains in reliability if a chart shows that the student experimented 5 times and graphed the different trials at 43, 39, 41, 45, and 37 seconds to select the "average time."

ELEMENTARY SCHOOL SCIENCE FAIR
JUDGING EVALUATION SHEET

Name of project: _____

Category entered: _____

Student name(s): _____

_____

Project identification number: _____

Teacher: _____

	Poor		Sufficient		Super
	1	2	3	4	5

INTERVIEW WITH STUDENT(S):

Knowledge:

Enthusiasm:

Oral presentation:

SCIENTIFIC THOUGHT:

Appropriate problem:

Posing the hypothesis:

Following the plan:

Gathering enough data:

Conclusions from data:

PRESENTATION:

Originality of idea:

Quality of exhibit display:

Clarity of exhibit:

COMMENTS:

Conclusion

Judges really set the tone for the culmination of the fair. If they try to set the student at ease, display enthusiasm, listen and respect what students have to say, offer honest but constructive suggestions, find aspects of the project that are genuinely deserving of praise, and communicate in terms that a young scientist can understand, they will have gone a long way in helping to make the elementary school science fair a success. Remember, fair number two will be twice as easy as your very first science fair!

Science fair participant _____

Title of entry _____

Great project!
Bill Jackson

I learned a lot from seeing your project.
Alex W.

WORDS OF WONDER!

Super graphs & charts!
Susan Gardner

Resources

Addresses frequently change. Some businesses and agencies close or take new names, and new businesses and agencies spring up. This resource list is up-to-date at the time of writing, but it is almost certain to be incomplete and to contain some inaccuracies at the time the reader sees it. Nevertheless, it should prove useful to students, parents, and teachers seeking information that might be useful in science fair projects.

Government agencies

Bureau of Mines
U.S. Department of the Interior
2401 E Street NW
Washington, DC 20241

Department of Agriculture
14th Street SW
Washington, DC 20250

Department of Commerce
14th Street SW
Washington, DC 20230

Department of Defense
The Pentagon
Washington, DC 20301

Department of Education
400 Maryland Avenue SW
Washington, DC 20202

Department of Energy
1000 Independence Avenue SW
Washington, DC 20585

Department of Health and Human
  Services
200 Independence Avenue SW
Washington, DC 20201

Department of the Interior
2401 E Street NW
Washington, DC 20241

Department of State
2201 C Street NW
Washington, DC 20520

Department of the Treasury
1500 Pennsylvania Avenue NW
Washington, DC 20220

Fish and Wildlife Service
U.S. Department of the Interior
2401 E Street NW
Washington, DC 20241

National Aeronautic and Space
  Administration
600 Independence Avenue SW
Washington, DC 20546

National Oceanographic and
  Atmospheric Administration
U.S. Department of Commerce
14th Street NW
Washington, DC 20230

Public Health Service
U.S. Department of Health and Human
  Services
200 Independence Avenue SW
Washington, DC 20201

U. S. Geological Survey
National Center
Reston, VA 22092

Societies and information agencies

Art, Science & Technology Institute
Dupont Circle Metro
2018 R Street NW
Washington, DC

Astronomy Program
University of Maryland
College Park, MD 20742

Department of Entomology
New Mexico State University
Las Cruces, NM 88003

Goddard Institute for Space Studies
2880 Broadway
New York, NY 10025

Jet Propulsion Laboratory
4800 Oak Grove Drive
Pasadena, CA 91109

National Audubon Society
950 Third Avenue
New York, NY 10022

National Space Science Data Center
Goddard Flight Center
Greenbelt, MD 20771

National Wildlife Federation
1412 16th Street NW
Washington, DC 20036

Philadelphia Academy of Natural
  Sciences
19th Street and Benjamin Franklin
  Parkway
Philadelphia, PA 19102

World Wildlife Fund
1255 23rd Street NW
Washington, DC 20037

Distributors of materials and supplies

Carolina Biological Supply Company
2700 York Road
Burlington, NC 27215

Childcraft Educational Corporation
20 Kilmer Road
Edison, NJ 08818

Delta Education, Inc.
P. O. Box M
Nashua, NH 03061

Denoyer-Geppert Company
5235 Ravenwood Avenue
Chicago, IL 60640

Edmund Scientific Company
Edscorp Building
101 E. Gloucester Pike
Barrington, NJ 08007

Fisher Scientific Company
4901 West Lemoyne
Chicago, IL 60651

JDR Microdevices
1224 S. Bascom Avenue
San Jose, CA 95128

NASCO Company
901 Janesville Avenue
Fort Atkinson, WI 53538

Radio Shack
(local stores)

Sargent-Welch Scientific Company
7300 N. Linder Avenue
Skokie, IL 60076

Science Kit, Inc.
777 E. Park Drive
Tonawanda, NY 14150

Showboard, Inc.
3725 West Grace Street, Suite 305
Tampa, FL 33607

Index

A

alarm, burglar, 85-87
animals, 5-6 (*see also* zoology)
  endangered species, 70-71
antacids, 146-147
ants, temperature effect on speed, 154-155
apples, measuring amount of juice in, 109-110
arch bridges, vs. beam bridges, 75-76
astronomy
  measuring diameter of sun, 113-115
  North Star, 147-148
awards, 169-171

B

background research paper, 2, 20-25, 32
bacteria, 127-128
  sterilization and, 128-129
bananas, ripening, 51-52
batteries, identifying poles, 143-144
beam bridges, vs. arch bridges, 75-76
beams
  balloon, 78-79
  position affects strength, 77-78
behavioral science (*see* health)
bibliography
  cards for, 23
  preparation, 8-9
binary calculator, making, 112-113
birds, food preferences, 157-158
botany, 40-57
  additional projects for, 53-55
  effect of soil depth on seed growth, 40-42
  leaf size, 43-44
  opening a tulip, 50-51
  plants seek light, 48-50
  popcorn seeds lift weight, 44-45
  ripening bananas, 51-52
  seeds need air to sprout, 45-46
  seeds take oxygen from air, 46-47
  smell affects taste, 52-53
  using different plant mediums, 42-43
  using light at night for plants, 47-48
bread, preservatives in, 123-124
bridges, beam vs. arch, 75-76
brine shrimp, 153-154
burglar alarm, 85-87

C

calculator, binary, 112-113
certificates, 169-171
Coanda effect, 82-83
coconuts, mold/bacteria in, 127-128
collections, 39
computer science (*see* mathematics)
contour map, 60-61
crystals, making, 64-65
cubes, 79-80

D

demonstrations, 39
display board, 10-12, 172
domes, 79-80

E

earth science, 58-74
  additional projects for, 71-73
  contour map, 60-61
  crystals, 64-65
  earth rotation speedometer, 58-59
  endangered species awareness, 70-71
  relative humidity
    evaporation, 65-66
    measuring, 66-67
  rock hardness, 59-60
  sedimentary rock formation, 63-64
  separating rocks/pebbles/sand, 62-63
  soil conservation, 69-70
  weather prediction accuracy, 68
electromagnetics, 141-143
encyclopedias, 21
endangered species, 70-71
engineering, 75-91
  additional projects for, 87-89
  balloon beams, 78-79
  beam bridges vs. arch bridges, 75-76
  beam position and strength, 77-78
  burglar alarm, 85-87
  Coanda effect, 82-83
  domes and cubes, 79-80
  liquid pressure power, 81-82
  noisy rooms vs. quiet rooms, 84-85
  triangles, 80-81
  wind pressure and vacuum, 83-84

About the author

Dr. Phyllis J. Perry has spent her entire adult life involved in various aspects of public education. She has taught in California, New Jersey, and Colorado, all the way from second grade to graduate school. She has been a curriculum specialist, educational programs specialist, director of talented and gifted education, and an elementary principal. Currently she is an educational consultant and freelance writer. Throughout her career, she has had a strong interest in science and in a multidisciplinary approach to education.

Dr. Perry is the author of nineteen books for children and adults including *A Teacher's Science Companion* (TAB Books, 1994). She has regularly been a judge at various school, district, and state competitions, including science fairs. Her experience in working with students, parents, teachers, school administrators, judges, and community sponsors has contributed to the practical, hands-on approach that she advocates in *Getting Started in Science Fairs*.